PRICING STRATEGIES
FOR SMALL BUSINESS

PRICING STRATEGIES FOR SMALL BUSINESS

Andrew Gregson, BA, MA, M.Sc (ECON)

Self-Counsel Press
(a division of)
International Self-Counsel Press Ltd.
Canada   USA

Self-Counsel Press acknowledges the financial support of the Government of Canada through the Book Publishing Industry Development Program (BPIDP) for our publishing activities.

Printed in Canada.

First edition: 2008

Library and Archives Canada Cataloguing in Publication

Gregson, Andrew
    Pricing strategies for small business / Andrew Gregson.
    ISBN 978-1-55180-797-3

    1. Pricing. I. Title.
HF5416.5.G735 2008   658.8'16   C2007-907685-8

Excerpts from the following books, articles, and organizations used with permission:

Harvard Business Review "Managing Price, Gaining Profit" HBS Publishing. September — October 1992.

Nagle, Thomas T.; Hogan, John. *Strategy & Tactics of Pricing: Guide to Grow More Profitably*, 4th Edition, © 2006. Reprinted by permission of Pearson Education Inc., Upper Saddle River, NJ.

Value promise from H&R Block used with permission.

"The Simple Truth About Why People Buy and Why They Don't Buy" used with permission of the Donald Cooper Corporation.

"How Can Appliance Parts and Service be Marketed Most Effectively?" Simon Fraser University MBA Research Project, Grant MacFarlane, 1982.

Winkler, John. Pricing for Results. ©1984 by Facts on File Publications, Inc., Imprint of Infobase Publishing. Reprinted with permission of the publisher.

Every effort has been made to obtain permission for quoted material and illustrations. If there is an omission or error, the author and publisher would be grateful to be so informed.

Self-Counsel Press
(a division of)
International Self-Counsel Press Ltd.

1481 Charlotte Road	1704 North State Street
North Vancouver, BC V7J 1H1	Bellingham, WA 98225
Canada	USA

CONTENTS

INTRODUCTION   xv

1 WHY IS PRICING IMPORTANT?   1

2 HOW TO KNOW IF YOUR PRICES ARE ALRIGHT   4

Is Price Just a Number?   5
What Makes Pricing Successful?   5
How Do You Know That Your Pricing Is Not Right?   11
Summary   13

3 TYPICAL PRICING METHODS IN USE TODAY   15

Classical Economics and Ye Olde Supply and
Demand Curves   15
Where to begin? Follow the Crowd!   19
WAG, SWAG and STICK Methods   20
Estimating Solutions   22
DIY (Do it Yourself) Estimating   24
The Trap of Customer-Driven Pricing   26

The Un-Trap of Customer Driven Pricing 27

Myth Busting: Market Share 29

Creating a Benchmark — Cost of Doing Business
Surveys 30

Risk and Return 31

5 Business Wreckers 36

Summary 36

4 POSITIONING FOR PRICE: THE ROLE OF THE
UNIQUE SELLING PROPOSITION 38

What is a Unique Selling Proposition (USP)? 38

How to Develop a Unique Selling Proposition 40

Franchises 47

Perceived Value 48

Who Is Your Customer? 48

So What, You Say? 49

Think Like a Customer 50

Summary 52

5 VALUE-DRIVEN PRICING 54

Pricing Down from Value versus Pricing Up from Cost 54

Contracting: A Recommended Strategy for Finding
the Customer's Buying Price 56

Retailing: Testing the water 56

Consulting 59

Service Businesses 61

Selling Industrially or Working with a
Professional Buyer 62

Distributing 62

Customer Behavior and Perceived Value 63

Reference Prices 64

Perceived Fairness 67

Gain-Loss Framing 69

Pricing on Purpose: Applying Value Pricing 71

Summary 72

6   COST-DRIVEN PRICING STRATEGIES   73

     Cost Approach Strategies   74

     Know Your Costs   77

     What Happens in a Strong Market?   81

     Summary   84

7   MARKETING AND SALES: WHERE YOUR PRICING DECISIONS BECOME REALITY   85

     Captive Product: Finding Value in Linked Products and Services   85

     Meeting the Price Objection   86

     Sales and Promotional Pricing   90

     Price Discrimination   95

     On Customer Behavior   98

     On Keeping Customers   100

     Sales Training   101

     Nine Guidelines for Presenting Your Price   104

     The Value of Persistence   106

     Pocket Price Banding   107

     Bundling and Unbundling   108

     Learning to Lose a Percentage of Sales   109

     The Winner's Curse   110

     And What of That Feeling That You May Have Left Money on the Table?   111

     Selling Best, Better, Good   112

     Using the Price Structure to Motivate Sales Staff   114

     Responding to a Price War   115

     Summary   116

8   PRICING MODELS   117

     Influence of Capacity Utilisation   118

     New Product Introduction   120

     Market Skimming   121

     Penetration Pricing   123

     Neutral Pricing   125

Activity-Based Costing (ABC) and Pricing 125

Marginal Cost Pricing 127

Summary 131

9 FINANCIAL ANALYSIS 132

Know Your Real Costs: Labor 133

Know Your Real Costs: Product 134

Know Your Real Costs: Overheads 135

Know Your Real Costs: Debt 136

Know Your Real Costs: Transaction Costs 137

The Impact of Discounting Prices 138

Goal Setting From the Top 142

Summary 147

10 DIAGNOSIS AND PRESCRIPTION: WHAT SHOULD I DO TO FIX MY PRICING? 148

Where Are You Not Paying Attention? 150

What Are You Giving Away for Free in Your Product That is Not Reflected in Your Prices? 152

Examine Your Customer Base. Do You Know What Your Customer Wants? 154

What Need Are You Satisfying for Which You Are Not Charging? 154

Check your Unique Selling Proposition 154

Test the Waters 155

Train Your Staff 155

Test Different Pricing Strategies 156

Going from Analysis to Action: Implementing a Price Increase 157

Summary 160

11 TRUE LIFE BUSINESS SCENARIOS: THE CASE STUDIES 161

Paying Attention to Pricing — Examples from Other Companies 161

Case Study
Pocket Price Banding — Castle Battery 163

Case Study
GENERIC Truck and Diesel Ltd. "Resetting
the Clock" 168

Summary 173

APPENDICES

I CALCULATING GROSS MARGIN VS. MARKUP 175

II FIXED AND VARIABLE COSTS 177

III ANALYZING YOUR FINANCIAL STATEMENTS 180

IV CALCULATING RETURN ON INVESTMENT 182

V CALCULATING LABOR COSTS 185

VI CALCULATING THE BREAKEVEN 187

VII CALCULATING HOW MANY EXTRA SALES
ARE NEEDED TO OFFSET A PRICE DECREASE 190

VIII READING LIST 195

IX WEBSITES 198

NOTICE

Laws are constantly changing. Every effort is made to keep this publication as current as possible. However, the author, the publisher, and the vendor of this book make no representation or warranties about the outcome or the use to which the information in this book is put and are not assuming any liability for any claims, losses, or damages arising out of the use of this book. The reader should not rely on the author or the publisher of this book for any professional advice. Please be sure that you have the most recent edition.

ACKNOWLEDGMENTS

I owe a huge debt of gratitude to a large number of people who have contributed wittingly or otherwise to this distillation of years of consulting work with small enterprises in Canada, the United States, and the Caribbean.

I have mentioned most of them throughout these pages, but two in particular deserve extra mention. First is my wife, Judith, who has perpetually encouraged and prodded me to make something of all my experience. She has been a fortress of confidence in my darkest moments.

And, I owe a debt to David Jenkins of Kelowna who read my 194 pages of drivel and pronounced it both readable and gently humorous.

Finally, I should thank Self-Counsel Press for taking an unbelievable chance with an unpublished author.

Andrew D. Gregson
Kelowna BC

INTRODUCTION
HOW TO GET THE MOST FROM THIS BOOK

I have written this book as a journey that seeks to explore the nooks and crannies of pricing, since it is a matter of great concern for small businesses. As such, it is long and involved.

If you have the leisure to read this book from page one to the appendices, then good for you. If, as I expect, you need to prepare a price for a customer tomorrow morning and want an answer now, then the outlines below will serve their purpose.

Although I would not normally recommend reading a book in reverse order, I believe there are instances where that is necessary — when an answer is needed tomorrow and reading the entire book and absorbing all its content is not possible.

Where to Begin If You Need to Solve a Pricing Problem Tomorrow Morning

- First, read Chapter 10, "Diagnosis and Prescription: What Should I Do to Fix My Pricing?"

- Read Chapter 9 on "Financial Analysis" and Knowing Your Real Costs.

Next, choose your industry.

If you are a contractor:

- Read "Estimating Solutions" in Chapter 3, page 22 and "DIY (Do It Yourself) Estimating," page 24.

- Read "5 Business Wreckers" in Chapter 3, page 36.

- Read "Risk and Return" in Chapter 3, page 31.

- Read Chapter 4 "Positioning for Price: The Role of the Unique Selling Proposition."

- Read "Contracting: A Recommended Strategy for Finding the Customer's Buying Price" in Chapter 5, page 56.

- Read about "Reference Prices" and "Gain Loss Framing" in Chapter 5, pages 64 and 69.

- Read "Nine Guidelines Presenting your Price" in Chapter 7, page 104.

- Read about "Bundling and Unbundling" in Chapter 7, page 108.

- Read "The Winner's Curse" in Chapter 7, page 110.

- Read Chapter 7 on "Learning to Lose a Percentage of Sales," page 109.

If you are in retailing:

- Read Chapter 4, "Positioning for Price: The Role of the Unique Selling Proposition."

- Read "Know Your Costs" in Chapter 6, page 77.

- Read "Retailing: Testing the Water" in Chapter 5, page 56.

- Read about "Selling Best, Better, Good" in Chapter 7, page 112.

- Read "Meeting the Price Objection" in Chapter 7, page 86.

- Read about "Bundling and Unbundling" in Chapter 7, page 108.

- Read about "Reference Prices" and "Gain Loss Framing" in Chapter 5, pages 64 and 69.

If you are in a service business:

- Read Chapter 4, "Positioning for Price: The Role of the Unique Selling Proposition."

- Read "Nine Guidelines for Presenting your Price" in Chapter 7, page 104.

- Read Chapter 7 on "Bundling and Unbundling," page 108.

- Read about "Reference Prices" and "Gain Loss Framing" in Chapter 5, pages 64 and 69.

If you are a manufacturer:

- Read all of Chapter 8, "Pricing Models."

- Read "Pricing Down from Value versus Pricing Up from Cost" in Chapter 5, page 54.

- Read Chapter 4, "Positioning for Price: The Role of the Unique Selling Proposition."

When you have overcome your immediate problems, then the entirety of Chapter 5 on "Value Pricing" is designed to expose you to the most current thinking about how to offer value in your pricing. If you have constructed a solid company with the basics outlined in the financial chapters, value pricing will make your company truly profitable and valuable.

1
WHY IS PRICING IMPORTANT?

The purpose of this book is to help small businesses with a neglected and vexing business problem: how to get prices right. They should be high enough so that the business makes a profit and yet low enough to keep customers coming through the door.

This is a neglected issue since most publications on this topic are for scholarly consumption, but judging by the current flurry of articles and books, pricing is becoming the next big business topic. Most of the books and articles I read for my research on pricing methods are struggling to find a framework for a new pricing "system."

This is also a neglected topic since most publications are directed at big businesses and draw most of their examples from huge corporations. There may be similarities in pricing logic between General Electric and the corner shop selling used clothing, but the similarities do not immediately rush out and take you by the hand.

Pricing is a vexing subject. Have you ever had customers respond badly to your pricing structure? Having a customer walk out or outright declare that your price is a "rip-off" is a horribly discouraging experience typically accompanied by a sick feeling in the pit of your stomach.

How do you get the pricing right, while in most markets there is competition from big-box giants like Wal-Mart or from chains bringing in Chinese-made goods, reducing your most profitable lines to a commodity that is bought and sold on the world stage based on price and nothing else?

"All too frequently, executives will complain about price problems and price pressures, but are these are rarely mere pricing problems. They usually deal with communication, branding, image, product, distribution, service excellence, segmentation, and other ill-conceived, ignored or poorly executed functions of a marketing strategy that isn't focused on value."[1]

When you are finished reading this book, you will have a working knowledge of many different pricing mechanisms. Moreover, you will have the tools to examine your own business to enable you to measure the impact of a new pricing scheme. But best of all, you will have many pricing options to choose from, options that will help you to set prices so that your business will clobber the competition.

When I began preparing this book for publication, I began with my consulting experience for small companies that had not yet got the basics right. For the most part my clients didn't grasp their real costs. Bidding on a job was something that happened on some distant planet in their imaginations, and bore no resemblance to the real world of their shop floors. A lot of my book is focused on helping small business owners to understand their costs and learn how to measure them.

As I have done my research for this book, I have dramatically expanded the value-added portion of pricing theory. In the past decade, pricing theory has reappeared in academic journals. The thrust of the research is no longer concerned with costs but with adding perceived value. The assumption is that the company knows its costs and as long as it covers its costs, it can proceed to add value by raising prices. I have used this information greedily.

If you read this book completely, you will discover that price is not purely a numbers game. In fact, it is difficult to get away from the notion that price reflects how a business delivers value to its customers. High prices ought to reflect high value. Low prices should

---

1. Baker. Ronald J. Pricing on Purpose. Creating and Capturing Value. John Wiley and Sons Inc. Hoboken, New Jersey. 2006

reflect commodities with little or nothing injected to add value. Therefore a large portion of this book encourages you, the reader, to review your business as a potential customer would; what value do you offer, how much is that value worth compared to your competition's offers, and is this transaction a fair trade?

Journeying down the path of price discovery entails looking into many dark and perhaps underperforming corners of the business. Therefore, this book touches on but does not exhaustively examine sales training, merchandising, estimating, motivation and marketing. In each area I have tried to keep the focus of the impact of pricing strategy on areas such as staff motivation, for example, and in reverse the impact of staff motivation on pricing structure.

As a business owner you only have to work half a day, and, better yet, you get to choose which twelve hours. I remember being a small business owner and how true this joke was for me. With that in mind, I have tried to recognize that the average business owner will get maybe five minutes of uninterrupted time to dip into this book and grab a useful idea, or perhaps the inspiration to read a whole chapter at night after business shuts down and everyone has gone to bed.

2
HOW TO KNOW IF YOUR PRICES ARE ALRIGHT

I argue throughout this book that a business owner must see his or her business as a struggle of perception. Customers strive to reduce everything to the most easily comparable state — apples to apples — and that means dollars per unit. A business must strive, on the other hand, to stop this from happening by presenting itself as pomegranates. If successful, then the customer cannot reasonably make a comparison on price only. Create a perception in the customer's mind that the business, product or service is different, and long-term business success can be yours. Create differences that actually have value in the mind of the customer. Throughout this book there are examples of perceived value and how it can be converted into better prices and better profits.

Before we can pursue that topic, however, we need to know if pricing is an issue in your business. In this chapter, I have highlighted a number of ways to see if your prices are too low. In the appendices, I have added sections on the math calculations to confirm this judgment and to help you measure the impact that pricing your product or service too low can have on your business.

Is Price Just a Number?

Price is the amount of money charged for a product or service for the benefit of receiving a product or service. The word "benefit" is emphasized because small business owners frequently lose sight of the relationship between benefits and the simple transaction of buying and selling.

An example is that of eating in restaurants. Most people eat in restaurants to celebrate an occasion, for "date night," or merely to take a break. The experience of eating out is the benefit, and the price tag cannot fairly be compared to the money spent if the same meal was cooked at home instead.

What Makes Pricing Successful?

Pricing is successful if:

- The company has a decent profit

- The owner is paid a reasonable wage

- The company and the owner pay their taxes

- The company has no difficulty finding the cash to pay the bills

- The company attracts the best quality customers who are willing to pay for the value added by the company

- The company generates a reasonable return on investment

- Bids on jobs are planned to leave no money on the table

What is a decent profit?

According to Statistics Canada, the average small company in Canada generates a profit before taxes of 5 to 10 percent of sales. This is not the only indicator of the health of a company but it is a good first step. With healthy profits, cash will be relatively easy to manage; Accounts Payable will be smaller than Accounts Receivable, the bills can be paid without having to hound customers who are just a few days late to cut you a check. If you miss a few weeks looking at the cash flow, it just doesn't matter too much.

I don't like averages; so what should the numbers be for my company?

Would you like to know what the median numbers are for your type of company? Wouldn't it be great to know if your percentage of profit or sales costs or even rent is "normal?" There are some ways to get that information. Quite often there are industry organizations that conduct "cost of doing business" surveys annually. By joining a trade association, you could get a survey and compare your own financial statements. Sometimes the previous year's survey is available at a small cost to give you a taste of the benefits of joining a trade association.

Paying the owner

Most importantly, a business exists to create profits after the owner is paid. Small business owners often lose sight of this objective in the sound and fury of everyday business, but a paycheck was clearly important when they began or bought the business. Getting the price right is the most important element in reaching the distant goal of financial security — either through profit generation or in getting a good price when selling the company.

What is a reasonable wage for the owner?

The simple test is an honest answer to the question: "Could I be earning more working for someone else?" If that answer is no, then the business pays you what you are worth in the open market. If the answer is yes, then your business needs work.

Or, suppose that you were planning retirement or became disabled. You could hire a manager in order to step back from the business and pay that person your wages. Would your pay be enough to attract and keep that person? If the answer is yes, then you are paying yourself a market value wage.

If you calculate the total hours you spend working and your wages are less than the wages of person who sweeps the floor, then you are not paying yourself enough.

Consider this scenario: You have a potential buyer across the desk from you. Of course, the price for the company is the topic. He or she wants to know how much he or she will earn and how much will be left over in the company. Is there a bottom line after his or her reasonable wage?

The company and the owner pay their taxes

Why is this important apart from not having CRA or the IRS chasing you? Recently I spoke with a business owner who wished to buy a house. His credit score was excellent and he had cash in the bank to manage the down payment. But because he had deliberately understated his personal and business income to reduce his taxes, his provable income was too low for the bank to consider loaning him the mortgage money.

In another instance, the owner of a company was trying to convince a potential buyer that the company was worth a great deal more than was shown on the books because the owner pocketed so much cash. But because the owner could not prove the cash flow either in his books or in his personal tax returns, the valuation of the company remained very low and no deal could be struck.

It is standard practice when preparing a company for sale to declare all revenues and take the tax hit during the last couple of years before the anticipated sale date. This bumps the revenue and the sale price. The new owner can employ whatever tax scheme he or she wishes after the cash has changed hands.

The business has no difficulty finding the cash to pay its bills

This would appear to be a "no-brainer" until you consider the colossal number of business owners who struggle to make payroll or find the money to pay for goods ordered to restock the shelves. Every time the price is too low, any minor expense that takes cash from the bank account — a sudden increase in Worker's Compensation rates, for example, or a fire, or a vehicle that is damaged by an employee — means there is a mad scramble for cash. If you have ever read any financial self-help books, you will remember that paying yourself first, or "saving for a rainy day," is the key to being able to sleep at night.

The business attracts the best quality customers who are willing to pay for the value added by the company

This is really the crux of the pricing issue. Good quality customers recognize the value in what your business offers and willingly write the checks. To get to that position, the business owner has to clearly articulate to the potential customer why his or her price has value for the customer's money.

Following are two examples of how perception can create "value for money."

EXAMPLE 1

Many years ago at a presentation in Chicago, we were shown two pictures. One showed an unshaven man with a bulging abdomen, wearing a dirty, torn t-shirt with a cigarette pack twisted up under the shirt's left arm. He wore dark glasses, had a cigarette hanging from his lower lip and was ignoring the camera.

The second picture showed a clean shaven man in a white lab coat looking right at the camera and clutching a clip board.

The presenter asked the room full of business owners what these two individuals did for a living. We replied that the first one had to be a plumber and the second a doctor.

In fact, both pictures were of the same person, just presented in a way that made one look more valuable than the other. Although there are jokes about doctors being paid less than plumbers these days, the point of the slide show was to demonstrate the importance of presentation to gain price and market share.

EXAMPLE 2

Plumbers have a bad, perhaps unearned, reputation for being slovenly and unreliable. But in the middle 1990s in Richmond, British Columbia, I came across a fellow who helped me with a toilet problem that arose after a visit from small members of the family, and was ultimately caused by the unauthorized presence of a toothbrush stuck in the toilet.

I had a very narrow window of opportunity, so Bob the plumber had to arrive at my house at 7:00 a.m. I would be away and my wife would have to let this stranger into our house at that early hour.

At precisely 7:00 a.m., Bob arrived and rang the doorbell. Bob was dressed in clean, pressed white overalls and presented his business card to my wife as she opened the door. When he finished fixing the toilet, he used his wet-dry vacuum to clean up the inevitable water spill and left a bill for me to pay.

Bob's Plumbing got a great review from my wife who proceeded to tell others about his services. How else could he stand out from the crowd? Wearing white overalls! Presenting a business card! Cleaning up all the water spills! Bob added value to his service, which in turn earned him valuable word-of-mouth promotion and the opportunity to further his business.

The business generates a reasonable return on investment

It is a good return if the $200,000 you have invested in your business gives you better returns than the bank would after taxes and your salary are paid. What this means is that if the cash you have invested in your business could be taken out and plunked into a bank account, would it earn more money than where it is currently in use?

EXAMPLE 3

If $200,000 in a nice, safe bank account generates 15 percent in interest revenue per year, it will give you a a tidy $30,000 a year income before taxes.

If the business has $200,000 of your money invested in it — your cash — and the annual profit before tax is less than $30,000, then you have a poor investment. It would be smarter to have that cash in a nice, safe bank account.

In comparing these two situations, of course, the owner would be drawing a wage and some benefits out of the company cash flow. We can safely assume here that with $200,000 stuffed into a bank account, the owner would still be working. We are only talking about the return on cash invested.

TABLE 1
WHERE IS YOUR MONEY BETTER EMPLOYED?

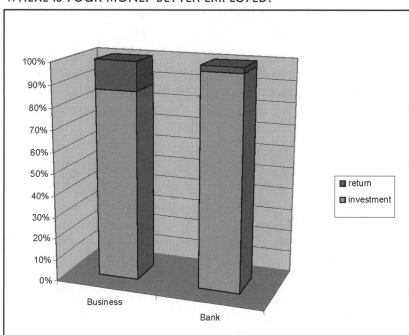

In fact this comparison can be used to decide the value of a business being sold or bought. Essentially, if you would earn more money just by having the cash in the bank and earning interest on it than you would by investing the same sum in the business, why would you invest in the business?

Bids on jobs are planned to leave no money on the table

Lots of companies bid on many jobs but plan for a predetermined profit, leaving no money on the table.

What this means is that the company plans to lose some bids deliberately and uses the ratio of bid-to-job to test prices every day. If prices are too high, then the ratio of lost bids climbs. If the company gets too many jobs, then it is time to raise prices.

Of course, knowing what the costs are in this scenario is critically important. If prices are generally sliding, then being able to cut costs quickly is important. So too is having flexible communications with the sales team so that cost-added features can be trimmed to bring prices into alignment.

If the company gets 100 percent of its bids, the price is likely too low and money is being left on the table. The services of the company are being sold as a commodity because the sales process has not found a way to find value and to make the company different from the competition. If you and the competition are identical then the only thing left to differentiate you is price.

How Do You Know That Your Pricing Is Not Right?

The Hamster Cage Syndrome

A company in the United States fabricated large metal tanks for several major industrial manufacturers. With two of its three major customers, it made a profit on the tanks. On the third contract, the largest of the three customers, the company lost money. The result was the company struggled to pay its bills but looked "sexy" because it had large revenue volumes. When a company is really busy but the dollars just flow through the bank account leaving nothing at the end of the year, the prices may be too low. Here the owner of the business runs and runs all day on the "wheel" like a hamster and goes nowhere.

But shouldn't you just cut costs and make a profit at lower prices?

Never pass up an opportunity to keep costs down. After all, the purpose of a business is to profit on the difference between selling price and costs.

However, every $1 earned from a price increase is $1 added to the bottom line. If your company typically generates a 5 percent profit before tax, every $1 saved in costs generates 5 cents on the bottom line. Better to find a way to increase your prices.

Two studies, one performed by McKinsey & Company and the other by A.T. Kearny, both consulting firms, demonstrated that a one percent improvement in the following areas resulted in net income increasing as shown in Table 2.[2]

2. Baker, Ronald J. Pricing on Purpose: Creating and Capturing Value. John Wiley and Sons Inc. Hoboken, New Jersey. 2006

TABLE 2
PRICING FUNCTION AND THE NET INCOME EFFECT
MCKINSEY AND A.T. KEARNEY STUDIES

	McKinsey Profit improvement	A.T. Kearny Profit improvement
Reducing Fixed Costs by 1 percent	2.7 percent	1.5 percent
Increasing Volume by 1 percent	3.7 percent	2.5 percent
Reducing Variable Costs by 1 percent	7.3 percent	4.6 percent
Increasing Price by 1 percent	11 percent	7.1 percent

Table 2 shows that driving sales volume is not as powerful a path to profit as increasing prices or reducing variable costs.

However, not all hamster cages are created equal. There was a business model in Vancouver, British Columbia, whereby all the products sold at rock bottom prices. The markup from landed cost (invoice cost plus shipping and handling, duty and all other costs attached to get the product onto shelves) covered the overhead and staffing.

The company profit component entered the picture only when staff hit very high sales targets that triggered a sales bonus from the manufacturer. The management had focused their time on negotiating these large bonuses and on driving the large volumes. While from the outside it looked like the business merely spun its wheels, in fact the owners had found a unique path to profit.

You hate your customers

Where price has been the sole focus of the company, it will attract only the most cost-conscious customers. These are the customers who want a discount on every item and ask for a discount even when the product is free. These are the customers who drive you crazy because they want a Cadillac job but only want to pay Pinto prices. These are the customers you hate to see coming through the door.

This type of company attracts only the price-conscious customers who do not really care about the quality of the job or the value the owner places on training employees, longevity in the business, or value-added features. You, as the business owner may care deeply about these features, but these customers place zero value on them.

What would your company be like if there was never any squabbling over prices and every customer beamed at you as they handed over a check? How would your staff react to being treated with respect for a job well done? What would the impact be on your reputation in the community?

Your company has a reputation for high prices

If your company has generated a reputation for high prices but has not successfully communicated the value to the customer, who sees only the sticker price and none of the benefits, you could have a problem. Unfortunately, this customer complains to his or her mother-in-law who mentions you to someone else and the ripple effect begins. Then, too few customers consider buying from your company and the business starves. This is the terror that stalks most businesses.

Summary

Your prices are probably too low if:

- Your company does not generate a profit and a liveable wage for the owner

- You hate your customers because they beat you up on price every day

- You get every job on which you bid

- You just spin on the wheel like a hamster but don't create profit

Your prices are probably alright if:

- The company has a decent profit

- The owner is paid a reasonable wage

- The company and the owner pay their taxes

- The company has no difficulty finding the cash to pay the bills

- The company attracts the best quality customers who are willing to pay for the value added by the company

- The company's return on investment is better than that of a bank account

- The bids on jobs are planned to leave no money on the table

- The company loses a pre-determined percentage of jobs to lower bids

In the appendices you will find calculations to help you decide whether, in your business, the problem of low profits is the fault of low prices or some other factor.

The next chapter concerns itself with existing pricing methods, how they work, and their downfalls. After that, the balance of the book is concerned with ways to raise prices by showing real and demonstrable value in what your company offers.

3
TYPICAL PRICING METHODS IN USE TODAY

I will call the following methods of pricing "default" because they appear to be in place in some businesses in the absence of a better method:

- Classical Economics and Ye Olde Supply and Demand Curves

- Follow the crowd

- WAG, SWAG and STICK methods

- Estimating solutions

- DIY (Do It Yourself) Estimating

- The Trap of Customer Driven Pricing

- The Un-Trap of Customer Driven Pricing

Classical Economics and Ye Olde Supply and Demand Curves

"In 1890, the English economist Alfred Marshall suggested that if a parrot were trained to answer 'supply and demand' to every question it was asked, the parrot could be given a degree in economics."[3]

3. Watts, Michael. The Literary Book of Economics. Intercollegiate Studies Institute. Wilmington, DE. 2004

If you studied Economics 101 at some point you probably learned about Alfred Marshall's supply and demand curves. The intersection of the two lines was meant to indicate where price levels would stabilize in a "perfect" marketplace.

TABLE 3
SUPPLY AND DEMAND

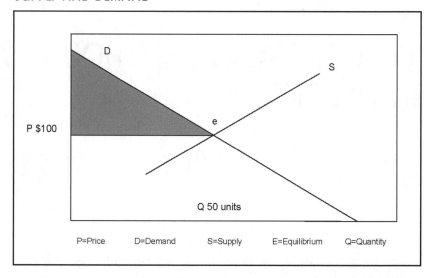

In Table 3, 50 units will sell at $100. Fewer than 50 units will sell at a price higher than $100 and more units will sell at prices lower than $100.

In Table 4, the point of equilibrium (e) is reached by the intersection of supply at 100 units and at a price of $33.

Large quantities in the presence of low demand means low prices. Supply will increase in the presence of high prices and therefore glut the market, forcing prices down. In reverse, a shortage of inventory in the presence of constant demand forces prices up. The whole system finds equilibrium where the two are balanced.

TABLE 4
EQUILIBRIUM

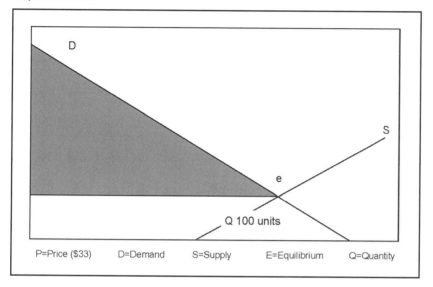

D				
				S
			e	
		Q 100 units		

| P=Price ($33) | D=Demand | S=Supply | E=Equilibrium | Q=Quantity |

The supply and demand relationship is used to justify the assumption that dropping prices will result in more sales. However, Alfred Marshall and Economics 101 always prefaced discussion of the graphs "in a perfect world." Of course, this perfect marketplace bears little resemblance to the day-to-day rough and tumble of running an auto-body shop, or roofing a house, or being a consultant. In fact, it bears no resemblance to highly visible and well-documented industries such as those of oil and diamonds. If you consider that a fistful of oil companies and a cartel (OPEC) control the price of gasoline, you will understand that the marketplace is distorted. Diamonds, until recently, were virtually a planet-wide monopoly of the De-Beers company founded in South Africa at the end of the 1800's. Not only did DeBeers control the mining and distribution, but also the cutting and retailing of the stones. Attempting to compete against DeBeers was like a modern version of Don Quixote charging at windmills on his horse.

Why is the theory so useless to the average small business owner?

Ninety-nine percent of small businesses have no way to test their pricing model daily. If you sold pork bellies on the Chicago Exchange, the price would move each day according to the supply from the pig farmers and the demand from the packing houses. But there is no fluid marketplace for hose reels, clothing, or pasta. That market-place function is undertaken by the business owner and his or her store. This means that knowing the theory of supply and demand is only good enough for the big picture and that uneven levels of local supply and demand will lead to price differences.

But the supply and demand theory is not dead. The availability of technology is having an impact on informing suppliers and cus-tomers, and flattening prices for commodity items. For example, a recent Economist article[4] noted the impact of cell phones on sar-dine fishermen in South India. Before the advent of cell phones, some 12 percent of the sardine catch was destroyed due to local market gluts. Afterwards, a fisherman with cell phone in hand could find the best price for his catch while at sea and then sail for the port with the highest prices. Prices reached a uniform plateau at 4 percent lower, on average, up and down the coast, and fishermen made 8 percent higher profit.

TABLE 5
WHY DO PRICES END IN 99¢?

Steven Landbsurg, The Armchair Economist, relates this anecdote about the origin of 99 cent pricing. In 1883, James Ritty and John Birch received a patent for inventing the cash register, which was quickly nicknamed the "Incorruptible Cashier." His invention came with that familiar bell sound of transaction being "rung" through. In 1884 John Patterson decided to buy both the company and the patent. He renamed the company the National Cash Register Company and improved the cash register by adding a paper roll to record sales transactions.

The cash register was a remarkable innovation that brought new control in the workplace. Not only did the register do simple arithmetic, it also kept a record of every sale on the paper roll. That's important if you think your employees might be stealing from you. You can scrutinize the paper tape at the end of the day and know how much cash should be in the drawer.

But there is one small problem with mechanical cash registers. They don't actually record every sale; they record only those sales that are rung up. If a customer buys an item with a price tag of $10 and hands the clerk a ten-dollar bill, the clerk can neglect to record the sale and slip the bill into his or her pocket. There is no record of the sale and the "theft" will appear as inventory shrinkage months later.

On the other hand, when a customer buys an item for $9.99 and hands the clerk a $10 bill, the clerk has to make change. This requires him to open the cash drawer, which he cannot do without ringing the unmistakable register bell. The bell announces the sale to the owner, who may be helping another customer, or who may be the back room doing the books. Ninety-nine cent pricing forces sales clerks to ring up sales and keeps them honest.

---

4. "Economics Focus: To do with the price of fish." Economist Magazine. May 12, 2007, p.84

In Canada, knowing that the number of housing starts has fallen will lead you to the inevitable conclusion that demand for lumber, hardware, and fixtures will likely suffer. It will suggest that finding a new market is important or that you need to find a way to out-manouever your competitors.

Knowing that the number of road accidents rises in winter, stabilizes during the shoulder seasons, and rises again in the summer due to vacation travel has an impact on your auto-body and paint shop business, your cash flow, and perhaps on where you set seasonal prices.

Supply and demand also affects businesses for their labor market. In Canada, where the labor market is so fluid, it seems the whole world knows the spread between statutory minimum wage rates and the bottom rung. In a downturn in the economy, the newspaper classified help-wanted ads shrink, and wage rates first flatten and then inevitably go down.

Fluidity also impacts contract bidding. It is a corollary of this type of business that the price is tested on each occasion because someone is asking for bids and your bid has to survive that test each and every time. Bid success is an important "metric" or measurement in business to determine whether prices should move up or down in response to the demand from customers and the supply of competitors.

Where to Begin? Follow the Crowd!

For most small businesses, the opening-day pricing regime starts with checking the competition's rates and prices, and then following the crowd. This is even the recommended strategy in many popular guides for small business. Merely following the crowd is all right but money is probably left on the table since the business is now just one of many, and the product or service is being priced like an undifferentiated commodity, e.g. pork bellies.

TABLE 6
PROHIBITION STORY

During the days of prohibition (in the U.S.), 25 of Chicago's top bootleggers were rounded up in a surprise raid. During their arraignment, the judge asked the usual questions, including the occupation of each suspect. The first 24 were all engaged in the same activity. Each claimed he was a real estate agent. "And, who are you?" asked the judge of the last prisoner. "Your Honor, I'm a bootlegger," he said. Surprised, the judge laughed and asked," How's business?" "It would be better," he answered, "if there were not so many realtors around."

The upside is that this strategy is simple and easy. You don't have all the time or money to spend developing a Unique Selling Proposition to get the full value for your services or product and you don't have to go out of your way to be better than all the rest. (For more about Unique Selling Propositions, see Chapter 4.)

The downside is that if everyone else is not making much money, neither are you.

EXAMPLE 4

Price matching: Does your company, as a matter of policy, match the prices of your competitors? Have you done this and not revisited these changes in your price list for so long that every item you now sell matches the price of the lowest retailer in town? Are your profits substandard?

For several years a Vancouver hardware supplier went down this road, until the overall performance of the company suffered. Changing price lists on the fly to respond to perhaps fleeting customer demand is easy. Remembering to put the prices back at some point is the hard part. So, margins fell and profits suffered.

WAG, SWAG and STICK Methods

In so many small businesses, pricing goods and services is often based on guesswork, the WAG method (Wild-Ass Guess). WAG is a term to describe an on-the-fly appeal to intuitive processes that lie outside of standard accepted scientific methodology. In other words, it's a plain, ordinary hunch. SWAG is a not very technical, time-honored acronym for Scientific Wild-Ass Guess, where there are some numbers to back up the guesswork. The STICK method means that every stick and nail is costed out.

WAG is best used only by those who have long experience in the industry or trade. This is an experience-based method for pricing where trial and costly errors have already taken place. If for the past ten years, it has cost $5,000 to renovate a bathroom then presumably it will always cost $5,000 to renovate a bathroom. Faced with creeping labor costs or perhaps sudden spikes in the price of plumbing fixtures, the WAG method, by not examining costs all the time frequently, makes price change sluggish and estimating unreliable. Faced with a new competitor in the market who is willing to undertake the same bathroom renovation for $3,500, the WAG method practitioner does not know how to respond properly. There is simply too much information that must be kept in the estimator's head to stay current and remain competitive yet profitable. Worse yet, estimators are human and tend to respond to the last comment they had from a customer. If that comment was negative because the customer thought the price was too high, then the price on the next job will drop. If the business owner is also the estimator, then the price might reflect not value to the customer or even costs, but the perilous state of the bank account at the time.

There is a deeper concern that the WAG skill is not easy to transfer because it cannot be written down. In most small businesses where the owner of the company is the estimator, this skill and knowledge is largely not transferable to employees or a new owner. This implies that the business will be undervalued when so much of the company's way of doing business is buried in the owner's head. When the time comes for the owner to retire, therefore, the price will reflect that hurdle and the potential for the value of the sale will likely be lower.

SWAG method, as the name implies, has some numbers to back up the experience-based approach. "OK, so that job will take four laborers five days to complete and I pay them $20 per hour. With labor cost at $3,200, add 1/3 for materials and then 1/3 for profit, that should be about it." This rough-and-ready method does not take into account travel time, overhead and management costs, payroll taxes, nor fudge factor in case things go wrong. This job might actually lose money.

There is an alternate SWAG method employed in some construction trades — the 1/3, 1/3, 1/3 method. In these estimates, the materials are costed very carefully and the total costs multiplied by three to give 1/3 for the labor (being of equal value to the materials) and leaving 1/3 for profit. As the reader may appreciate, this is a scary method. Paint costs less than granite countertops so the pricing structure can get skewed. As a rule of thumb this method has its uses, but as a backup to any other method of estimating rather than the entire methodology. In other words, if your detailed method and the 1/3 method give the same answer, you can be reasonably certain that your pricing is near enough to the correct price to prevent any nasty surprises.

The STICK method is the name given to the clumsy and time-consuming method of working out the cost of each and every nail, foot of strapping, two by four, pot of paint and labor to the nearest 15 minutes to arrive at a total cost. It is very intensive and does not produce a better sales response from customers. In fact, the delay in getting quotes back to customers can be the sole deciding issue in whether or not your company gets the job.

The STICK method is, in fact, an adaptation of industrial manufacturing cost accounting methods to the businesses of service providers and custom builders. It can take place on paper, and I have also seen some very elaborate spreadsheets meant to cope with a vast amount of information. The advantage to having gone to the trouble of detailing every aspect of this "virtual build," is that if and when the customer says "Okay," you have a bill of materials for the purchasing department and a detailed plan for the carpenters.

There are two principal disadvantages to the STICK method. First is the speed factor. If you are an estimator for a home renovator for example, you must make at least two visits to the site and perhaps several phone calls before you have an answer. And there is always the feeling among business owners and estimators I have talked with that some estimates are just a waste of time, but they must go through this drawn-out procedure just because they were asked for a quote.

Second is that, having committed so much time and effort to the quote, the price is not easily altered to reflect customer expectations. In other words, if the quote is $7,000 and the customer's budget does not extend beyond $5,000, you cannot easily and quickly find the savings to meet the price expectation. There is simply too much information to alter the quote simply and easily. The only line item that can easily be altered is the bottom line, and doing so may mean the job makes no money.

Estimating Solutions
Estimating software

There are an increasing number of industry-related packages for estimators. Many of them utilize the power of computers and spreadsheets to manipulate large quantities of information without error. This is the STICK method on amphetamines.

The best place to look for packages is in trade magazines and other publications. If you choose this approach to doing estimating systematically and correctly, it is always good practice to have a test run of the software: Entering data from an existing quote to see if the numbers work. Beware country-specific programs that do not allow for certain taxes.

If the software is truly sophisticated, then it will also create a bill of materials for your purchaser, saving you hours of time.

Estimating books — OEM and industry service providers

Significantly, there are companies that provide estimating in a more packaged form that gets the final number quickly. The one with which I have a working familiarity is focused specifically on the construction trades.[5]

They have created formulae into which you plug the square feet, height over normal, number of windows and/or doors, and utilise either economy, medium, or high value materials. In a few minutes, out pops a number which is then multiplied against a regional factor to arrive at a selling price. It keeps track of cost differentials through regional surveys which translate to a factoring number that you plug in to give a final price.

Similarly, the auto-body industry gets books from the manufacturers detailing how long it will take for a fender to be straightened or a side panel to be hammered out. From this it is easy to determine what your costs are going to be and to apply a markup factor. Typically, the auto-body people use this information to apply standard rates and then encourage their technicians to improve upon those numbers. If they accomplish in 24 hours what the book says will take 32 hours, the price does not change but the costs do.

If your industry has a guide like this, get your hands on it and use it as a guideline to keep your costs and pricing under control. When price and costs are under control, you can play with them to find higher profits, and teach these methods to business partners and employees. The value in the business increases through having these systems in place.

---

5. Walt Stoeppelwerth, Estimator Books and Software, www.hometechonline.com.

DIY (Do it Yourself) Estimating

You can do it yourself. If the industry you serve has no package to offer you, you can create an estimator package to standardize your costs as follows:

- First list all of the steps in the information gathering stage. What are the types of material, size, finish, and availability? List all the extras. What does your customer expect?

- Then list how you currently price jobs focusing on the steps that must be taken. Do you always strip the roof before installing new tile? Do you always begin with cutting the pipe into 12 foot lengths? Do the raw materials always have to be sandblasted first?

- Apply costs to each step.

- Apply your markup factor to get to a selling price.

- And now the most important step — the virtual trial run. Review previous jobs that worked out well and where you made money. Punch in all those numbers.

All these steps could be taken by a software developer and can be incorporated into a spreadsheet program or kept on paper.

Now comes the hard part. As you use the paper system or the spreadsheet, you have to review and refine and update as you go. If you find that allowing 45 minutes for sandblasting is too little now that old Fred has retired and young Tom is doing it, then you have to change the value for the minutes or risk losing profit. As the price of material changes or new methods or equipment is used, the procedure will need to be renewed. This is, in effect, the SWAG method perfected, because you are reusing a body of knowledge and information, then you are building and adding new factors to it as you go.

For an example of creating a DIY estimator for your business (first stage estimating guidelines for a roofing company), see Table 7.

TABLE 7
DIY ESTIMATOR

New Construction: labor only

Roof Pitch	3/12 : 5/12	$X.00 per square of roof tiles
	6/12 : 9/12	$XX.00 per square of roof tiles
	10/12 :12/12	$XXX.00 per square of roof tiles

Variables:

Extra $10.00 per square of roof tiles if the roof has more than one roof line
Extra $ 5.00 per square of roof tiles if more than two (2) stories

Remove & Replace single layer asphalt roof: labor only

Roof Pitch	3/12 : 5/12	$X.00 per square of roof tiles
	6/12 : 9/12	$XX.00 per square of roof tiles
	10/12 :12/12	$XXX.00 per square of roof tiles

Variables:

Extra $20.00 per square for each additional layer of existing roof to be removed
Extra $10.00 per square of roof tiles if the roof has more than one roof line
Extra $ 5.00 per square of roof tiles if more than two (2) stories

Conversion cedar to asphalt re-sheet with plywood: labor only

Roof Pitch	3/12 : 5/12	$X.00 per square of roof tiles + $10.00 per sheet of plywood installed
	6/12 : 9/12	$XX.00 per square of roof tiles + $10.00 per sheet of plywood installed
	10/12 :12/12	$XXX.00 per square of roof tiles + $10.00 per sheet of plywood installed

Variables:

Extra $10.00 per square if the roof has more than one roof line
Extra $ 5.00 per square if more than two (2) stories

Extras:

Flashing installation:	$ 3.00 per linear foot
Ice & water installation:	$15.00 per roll
Siding remove & reinstallation:	$ 5.00 per square foot
Venting installation:	$ 5.00 per linear foot

Remove & Replace single layer asphalt roof: supply & install

Roof Pitch	3/12 : 5/12	$X.00 per square of roof tiles
	6/12 : 9/12	$XX.00 per square of roof tiles
	10/12 :12/12	$XXX.00 per square of roof tiles

Variables:

Extra $20.00 per square for each additional layer of existing roof to be removed
Extra $10.00 per square of roof tiles if the roof has more than one roof line
Extra $ 5.00 per square of roof tiles if more than two (2) stories

TABLE 7 — CONTINUED

Cedar to asphalt shingle conversion – re-sheet with plywood: supply and install		
Roof Pitch	3/12 : 5/12	$X.00 per square of roof tiles + $10.00 per sheet of plywood installed
	6/12 : 9/12	$XX.00 per square of roof tiles + $10.00 per sheet of plywood installed
	10/12 :12/12	$XXX.00 per square of roof tiles + $10.00 per sheet of plywood installed

Variables:

Extra $10.00 per square if the roof has more than one roof line
Extra $ 5.00 per square if more than two (2) stories

Torch-on roofing (tar and gravel): Remove and replace, supply and install

$XXX-$XXX per square foot depending on level of difficulty (example: if a roof has many protrusions or obstacles, it is more difficult and would cost more)

With more tinkering and constant upgrades the above can be made into a comprehensive price list that covers the basics and some of the eventualities. All that is needed in order to prepare a quote on site is a tape measure and a calculator.

The Trap of Customer-Driven Pricing

So, should the owner just ask the customer what he or she wants to pay for the product or service and then sell it at that price? No. It is wise to pay attention to customers but unwise to be swayed by anecdotal evidence, even if it is firsthand. Only numbers count and having the statistical evidence to back up customer comments is the only valid method I know.

Suppose you invent a nifty new technological solution to a computer-networking problem that plagues most small companies. Should you decide to take this "magic widget" to the market and ask customers what they will pay for it, you will get a wide variety of answers from zero to hundreds. After all, the customer has never seen anything like it before. How do you price it using the concepts we've discussed?

This example is laced with a key misconception. You are not selling the widget, you are selling the solution. And if the problem your widget promises to fix amounts to hundreds of dollars worth of frustration, downtime, and lost productivity every year, then the widget sells for a multiple of that number regardless of its production cost.

Just asking what the customer would be willing pay for the item is not enough. As a wily business owner, you must know what problem the customer is buying your product or service to solve.

Again, if the product is a chop saw and the weekend warrior is in your store, the salesperson's first question has to be, "What project are you planning?" If the project is crown moldings, the cheapest machine will simply not be satisfactory.

"The job of sales and marketing is not simply to process orders at whatever price customers are currently willing to pay, but rather to raise customers' willingness to pay to a level that better reflects the product's true value … Low pricing is never a substitute for an adequate marketing and sales effort."[6]

The Un-Trap of Customer Driven Pricing

Consider for a moment turning this argument on its head and giving yourself a new vision for your business.

What would happen if you started with the price at which your research shows you can sell Product X? You are certain of the volumes because you have a purchase order in your hands.

Can you make or produce Product X for that price and have a profit after all costs are taken into account? One of history's greatest industrialists did exactly this.

What Ford put first: The profit lure of mass production obviously has a place in the plans and strategy of business management, but it must always follow hard thinking about the customer. This is one of the most important lessons that we can learn from the contradictory behavior of Henry Ford. In a sense Ford was both the most brilliant and the most senseless marketer in American history. He was senseless because he refused to give the customer anything but a black car. He was brilliant because he fashioned a production system designed to fit market needs. We habitually celebrate him for the wrong reason, his production genius. His real genius was marketing. We think he was able to cut his selling price and therefore sell millions of $500 cars because his invention of the assembly line had reduced the costs. Actually he invented the assembly line because he had concluded that at $500 he could sell millions of cars. Mass production was the result — not the cause — of his low prices.

---

6. Nagle, Thomas T., Hogan, John, *Strategy and Tactics of Pricing: Guide to Grow More Profitably*, 4th edition, 2006. Reprinted by permission of Pearson Education Inc., Upper Saddle River, NJ

Ford repeatedly emphasized this point, but generations of production-oriented business managers have refused to hear the lesson he taught. Here is his operating philosophy as he expressed it:

"Our policy is to reduce the price, extend the operations, and improve the article. You will notice that the reduction of price comes first. We have never considered any costs as fixed. Therefore we first reduce the price to the point where we believe more sales will result. Then we go ahead and try to make the prices. We do not bother about the costs. The new price forces the costs down. The usual way is to take the costs and then determine the price; and although that method may be scientific in the narrow sense, it is not scientific in the broad sense, because what earthly use is it to know the cost if it tells you that you cannot manufacture at a price at which the article can be sold? But more to the point is the fact that, although one may calculate what a cost is, and of course all of our costs are carefully calculated, no one knows what a cost ought to be. One of the ways of discovering … is to name a price so low as to force everybody in the place to the highest point of efficiency. The low price makes everybody dig for profits. We make more discoveries concerning manufacturing and selling under this forced method than by any method of leisurely investigation."[7]

As you examine the methods to analyze your business in later chapters and the appendices, you will discover that starting at the desired end product and working backwards generates some fascinating insights. Ford explained that he started from a price and worked backwards to make the product fulfill the profit objective.

Can you do this in your business? Yes. Customer expectations can be managed at the marketing and sales levels. This drives volumes. Can you buy the ingredients or raw materials at better prices? Can you find a smarter way to make the finished product?

If you are going to have pricing driven by customer expectations, be the market leader. Have more market share than the next competitor. Sell at 7 percent to 10 percent above the rest of the market and commit a large chunk of that extra money to marketing and advertising to keep you on the top of the brand wagon. Then back up your promises with a quality product and great service. It sounds easy, if you say it quickly.

---

7. Henry Ford. My Life and Work (New York, Doubleday, Page & Company, 1923. Quoted by Theodore Leavitt in "Marketing Myopia," Harvard Business Review No. 75507. September-October 1975).

The only sustainable way to increase relative profitability is by achieving a competitive advantage that will enable you to increase sales and margins. In short, the goal of a strategic plan should not be to become bigger than the competition (although that can happen), but to become better. Such positive-sum competition, rather than undermining the profitability of an industry, constantly renews it.

Myth Busting: Market Share

It is a common mistake to expect to grab market share by dropping a price. Not only do marketers think this, but so do salespeople in the hope of getting a sale to boost their numbers. But market share precedes profitability, not the other way around.

A common myth in the marketing world is that market share is the key to profitability. Robert Jacobson and David Aaker in their 1985 article in the Journal of Marketing, "Is Market Share All That It's Cracked Up To Be?" examined this pervasive myth. If you consider the companies on the planet that have dominated their industries that would mean some gigantic companies like GM, Ford, and Philips should also be hugely profitable. The contrary is true. In fact, these companies have experienced significant financial setbacks, especially as of late.

Nevertheless some large companies with huge market share command huge profits, like Microsoft. Why? Perhaps it's because both profitability and market share are caused by the same underlying source of business success; a sustainable competitive advantage in meeting customer needs and doing so more efficiently. When a company has a competitive advantage that makes it stand out from the crowd, it can earn higher margins due to either higher prices or a lower cost of production.

A strong competitive advantage, if sustainable, also discourages competitors from targeting the company's customers or from effectively stonewalling its attempts to expand. In reverse, a less efficient company with large market share would find itself targeted by lean and mean competitors ready to slice off chunks of market share with price competition. What this means is that market share is not the path to huge profits, but rather a further indicator of a well-run company.

Unfortunately, the received wisdom among many managers is the contrary and they perceive a cause and effect, and seek to change that by engaging in a price war to drive out competitors. Much of the time the hoped-for profits never materialize. In fact, profits take a huge hit in the company instigating a price war.

It follows, therefore, that the objective of a plan for company growth should not be to achieve sales volumes but to create and sustain a competitive advantage. Look at the two exemplars of this. Wal-Mart entered the retail market long after Sears. Wal-Mart was a hugely profitable company long before it came to dominate the market and then challenge Sears. Sears, as market leader, reported poor profits for decades, making it vulnerable to Wal-Mart's aggression.

A strategic plan created to gain market share by dropping prices or accepting higher costs like free delivery is likely doomed to failure. The collapse of margins makes companies vulnerable to ruthless and deep-pocketed competitors. When they drop prices even more steeply, the instigator of a price war may not be able to follow easily.

Rather, it is important to realize that the connection is between profits and real competitive advantage. If the competition cannot follow, then prices are safe, volumes will grow, and profits will soar.

Creating a Benchmark — Cost of Doing Business Surveys

Average is exactly that: Average. Fifty percent are better than you and fifty percent are worse.

Where to begin? Know where the average is and rise above it!

A simple strategy to establish your benchmark and to know whether your company has good pricing or bad is to join an association and get their cost of doing business surveys. The annual surveys are sold to the membership and show line by line the costs for staffing, commissions, rent, overheads, and even owner remuneration expressed as a percentage of total sales. Even a year-old survey is a wonderful source of information to benchmark your business.

If the cost of goods is 35 percent at your establishment and the typical cost of goods in Canada[8] or your region is 29 percent, your prices are low, or wastage is high or you have dishonest employees, and that might explain some of the company's financial difficulties.

All of the sales in Table 8 are expressed as percentages of the gross sales. If your financial statements do not currently show each line as a percentage of sales and last year's figures (year-on-year or month-on-month) then ask your bookkeeper.

Risk and Return

Very often businesses will attach a tariff to flow through charges to cover the costs of paperwork and gain a little profit. It seems like a good idea that if you provide an outside contractor for a job that you should add 10 percent onto the bill. Many times it works. All of the time there is a risk of the job going sideways. There is a risk attached to these returns and it needs to be considered carefully and wisely.

Suppose that you had the chance to cut a check for $1,000 that represented your entire out-of-pocket expenses. For the $1,000 you might have an option to purchase a house for $270,000 but the house is really worth $340,000. Would you do it?

The ratio of risk-to-reward is low. The risk is the non-refundable $1,000 deposit taken from your bank account. The house will never evaporate and in most cases not depreciate. Moreover, you are buying the house at less than list value. The reward factor is measurable.

Let us suppose on the other hand that you had a chance to cut a similar check for $1,000, in return for the chance to buy stocks in a company about which you knew nothing except that the promoter told you it would hit the heavens.

The risk-to-reward ratio is high and without doing a little bit of homework, you should probably feel queasy about signing that check.

---

8. Statistics Canada released a study in 1997 that showed 25 percent of inventory shrinkage was due to theft, 25 percent was due to clerical errors, and the final 25 percent was due to vendor fraud.

TABLE 8
PROFITABILITY RATIOS

	All companies	Benchmark	More than $1 million	Your results
Profitability Ratios				
Direct Cost Percentage	29.22 percent	25.66 percent	16.05 percent	29.16 percent
Gross Margin	70.68 percent	74.34 percent	83.95 percent	70.84 percent
Selling, General and Administrative	62.69 percent	56.39 percent	26.47 percent	63.73 percent
Operating Profit Margin	5.61 percent	17.22 percent	11.15 percent	7.11 percent
Net Profit Margin	4.19 percent	16.60 percent	7.83 percent	1.58 percent
Owner's Discretionary Profit Margin	11.61 percent	29.38 percent	13.48 percent	8.39 percent
Owner's Discretionary Profit Dollars	$76,502	$231,441	$211,770	$177,501
Productivity Ratios				
Total Revenue Per Employee	$66,606	$98,038	$68,791	$100,699
Staff Cost Per Employee	$25,562	$26,150	$27,182	$30,440
Staff Cost Percentage	29.29 percent	20.29 percent	40.87 percent	27.35 percent
Rental Income to Net Rental Assets	2.61	2.07	3.56	1.25
Gross Margin Return on Rental Equip	2.30	1.92	3.11	1.41
Median Total Revenues	$602,972	$779,770	$1,605,076	$2,114,687
Financial Position				
Total Revenues to Assets	1.45	1.24	1.74	1.17
Return on Assets	17.39 percent	36.50 percent	20.72 percent	9.82 percent
Return on Investment	1.25 percent	54.93 percent	68.90 percent	217.94 percent
Debt to Worth	1.73	0.41	1.47	21.21

How does this apply to pricing? Having a keen perception of the downside of a contract may help you make shrewd business decisions rather than fatal ones. At the beginning of my career I was told that a bad business decision is one you cannot back away from gracefully. An appreciation of the risk may persuade you not to change the overall value of the package of goods and services but rather to unbundle them to reflect your risk and rewards.

In other words, how can you legitimately give value to your customer in providing services or products outside your normal course of business and see some of the profit for doing so hit your bank account? At the same time, how can you place a wall between you and the outside provider so that his or her poor performance or bad luck does not have a disastrous impact on your business?

EXAMPLE

During the hot property market years in British Columbia, a kitchen design company employed the standard business model of selling an entire kitchen design, buying the cabinets, installing the cabinets, and putting a markup of a few points on the cabinets and the installation. The cabinet manufacturer demanded 100 percent of the cabinet price up front and was frequently late, especially for small customers like my client.

On first examination, it appears that the designer would have a $6,000 job profit on a $35,000 job — a 17 percent profit margin. On a job sheet or a profit and loss statement, it would be difficult to find fault with this model. However, when you considered the cash flow and the market circumstances the picture changed horribly.

First, the dollars paid to the manufacturer for the cabinets — $20,000 — came from the customer's initial deposit. The entire customer deposit had been used to buy the cabinets.

In order to complete the job, the company had to use its own cash reserves to cover the cost of installation and design. This was a cash flow nightmare for my client. When the cabinet manufacturers did not deliver on time (a frequent occurrence); or delivered only a portion of the cabinets ordered — almost 90 percent of the time — the customers were understandably unhappy. If the customers demanded their money back — and they did — the company did not have the cash reserves to comply.

The company fought to get around this difficulty; upon completion a significant number of customers refused to pay the 10 percent holdback on the entire job — $3,500 or 58 percent of the entire anticipated profit.

The risk-return ratio was wrong for the market circumstances due to the unreliability of the cabinet makers.

In remedying this problem, the business model had to be turned on its head by unbundling the transaction and getting the profit paid first.

Initially, the customer paid the company for a kitchen design. This translated into $8,000 in revenue that paid for the design and overheads. All of the profit to be expected from this transaction was therefore paid up front, plus $2,000 for future costs.

Then the customer was introduced to the manufacturer from whom they bought the cabinets directly. Blame for late or incomplete deliveries came home to roost with the manufacturer and the designer could commiserate but never had to take the blame.

When the time came for the installation, it was paid by the customer to the company and the company paid the installer.

Even better, the design company got a sales commission from the manufacturer.

From a price point of view, the cost to the customer did not change. However, perception of added value did change. In the first place, they believed the designer was getting them the manufacturer's best price and since they paid the manufacturer directly, they were not being "taxed" by the designer. The customer paid for performance and the designer that designed the kitchen and was paid. When the cabinets arrived, the installer was paid. Even with a normal holdback, the risk to actual profit was minor.

TABLE 9
KITCHEN DESIGN EXAMPLES

Company cost of the cabinets	$20,000	
Installation at cost	$4,000	
Design at cost	$5,000	
Total cost of kitchen renovation	$29,000	
Markup on the cabinets	$2,000	10 percent
Markup on installation	$1,000	25 percent
Markup on design	$3,000	60 percent
Total expected profit	$6,000	
Total price of kitchen renovation	$35,000	
Customer deposit	$20,000	57 percent
Anticipated profit on this job	$6,000	17 percent
10 percent holdback by the customer	$3,500	58 percent of total profit
AFTER		
Company cost of the cabinets	$0	
Installation at cost	$4,000	
Design at cost	$5,000	
Total cost of kitchen renovation	$9,000	
Commission on the cabinets	$2,000	
Markup on installation	$1,000	25 percent
Markup on design	$3,000	60 percent
Total expected profit	$6,000	
Total price of kitchen design & installation	$15,000	
Customer deposit	$13,500	
Anticipated profit on this job	$6,000	67 percent
10 percent holdback by the customer	$1,500	25 percent of total profit
Customer Pricing		
Old way		
Total cost	$ 35,000	
New way		
Cost of design & installation	$ 15,000	
Cost of cabinets	$ 20,000	
Total cost	$ 35,000	

So, in your business, are you risking large amounts of cash on deals that stand a chance of going sideways? What is the realistic risk? And how do you avoid it?

5 Business Wreckers

In the interests of exploding all the pricing myths I could find, the following carefully places dynamite under some people that can distract an owner from making the best decisions for his or her business.

Ways to identify a business wrecker[9]:

- Business wreckers imagine all business rumors to be true. They believe that all competitors are undercutting them and believe every customer who tells them they are too expensive.

- Business wreckers believe that if sales go down, it is the fault of high prices. They fail to look at the total industry numbers or share of the market the company is taking.

- Business wreckers always concentrate upon some prices only, to the exclusion of others. They also believe that costs are the only factor influencing prices.

- Business wreckers hide in a crisis. They believe that the crisis will blow over without them doing anything about it and that the price they have is the fair price.

- Business wreckers are often honorable people who believe that there is a moral price and a moral profit. As such they are willing to forgo large profits but have no recovery plan against awful losses.

Summary

Wake up!

Examine the ways you do your pricing and estimating. They can be improved. Absolutely!

There is no perfect market with demand perfectly balanced by supply. Even the advent of the Internet and its ability to convey detailed information to millions of customers and clients has not yet altered the supply and demand scale. So if your response to your business woes is supply and demand, then remember Alfred Marshall

---

9. Winkler, John. Pricing for Results. ©1984 by Facts on File Publications, Inc., Imprint of Infobase Publishing. Reprinted with permission of the publisher.

said that if you could teach a parrot to reply "supply and demand" to every question, you could bestow an economics degree upon it.

Following the crowd by pricing like all the rest is a recipe for the lazy spiral of mediocrity. You can do better. You can get a better price than your competitors. But it will take some examination of your business and pricing methods.

Estimating methods like WAG, SWAG and STICK are clumsy and unprofessional. There are better ways, with the expenditure of either time or cash, to develop methodical estimates with a relationship to cost and get the right price in minutes, not hours. And to get the right price each time in response to your customer's needs. And be able to teach this method to staff so that someone can buy your business an expect it to make a profit.

Driven crazy by your customer? Perhaps you are the tail wagging the dog instead of the dog wagging the tail? This is a trap where you let customers dictate the price. The business wreckers mentioned in this chapter are all too common. If you drive them out of your company they may concentrate on your competitors. However, listening to the customer can give you valuable insight into the motivations and value placed on your goods and services. But be careful and measure it. Anecdotal evidence is a business wrecker.

And speaking of measuring, you cannot get a better baseline to see where you need to improve than buying a cost of doing business survey for your industry. Armed with these one or two pages, you can examine your business item by item and line by line to see how well you compare. Better than average? Good. Keep up the good work. But never settle for mediocrity. Below average? What can you do to improve?

This chapter was about exploding the complacent attitudes about pricing and estimating that build and maintain mediocre businesses. These businesses consistently underperform, and at the same time cause stress for the owners. The pricing methods described here disguise the fact that the business has not clearly thought through its position in the marketplace; how the business can get top dollar for its services; and how to communicate this value-for-money argument to the customer. The next chapter describes this process.

4
POSITIONING FOR PRICE: THE ROLE OF THE UNIQUE SELLING PROPOSITION

"A common mistake made by pricing managers is to assume that their objective is to set a price for the product rather than the customer segment."[10]

The purpose of this chapter is to introduce the concept of the Unique Selling Proposition. Knowing how to define, understand and utilize the concept is the first step in knowing how to improve your prices. After all, if your business is the same as all the others — and why should it be? — then you will compete only on price and price will inevitably grind down to the lowest common denominator.

What is a Unique Selling Proposition (USP)?

In his book *Reality in Advertising*, Rosser Reeves (Chairman of the Board at Ted Bates & Company) gives the precise definition as it was understood at his company:

- Each advertisement must make a proposition to the customer: "Buy this product, and you will get this specific benefit."

- The proposition itself must be unique — something that competitors do not, or will not, offer.

10. Nagle, T.E. and Hogan, John. *Strategy and Tactics of Pricing: Guide to Grow More Profitably,* 4th edition, 2006. Reprinted with permission of Pearson Education Inc., Upper Saddle River, NJ.

- The proposition must be strong enough to pull new customers to the product.

However, Reeves warns against forming an USP based on what he calls "The Deceptive Differential" — a uniqueness that is too small or too technical for customers to observe the differences in.

Some good current examples of products with a clear USP are:

- Head & Shoulders: "You get rid of dandruff"
- Olay: "You get younger-looking skin"
- Red Bull: "You get stimulation of body and mind"

Some unique propositions that were pioneers when they were introduced:

- FedEx: "Next-day delivery by 10:00 a.m."
- M&Ms: "The milk chocolate melts in your mouth, not in your hand"

A good USP has the following characteristics:

1. It highlights a specific benefit to be had from using the company or buying the product.
2. It is unique — something competitors do not or will not offer.
3. It is strong enough to pull new customers in.
4. It is short.
5. It paints a mental picture.
6. The differences highlighted are substantial.

Sample of a good USP

Domino's Pizza: "You get fresh, hot pizza delivered to your door in 30 minutes or less — or it's free."

This is a good USP because it fulfills all six of the above criteria. The benefit is reliable and fast delivery so the pizza is hot when you get it. Most pizza joints still will not give an "or it is free" guarantee. The free aspect draws customers who might not otherwise experiment with your company. It is only a few words. You can just see the pizza delivery guy standing on your doorstep with a steaming pizza in the box. The difference between this company and the competition is the reality that pizza often arrives lukewarm and late.

Sample of a bad USP

"Guaranteed, Quality Service at Fair Prices."

This is a bad USP because it fulfills one criteria; it is short. It does not paint any mental picture of a benefit. It is far from unique. Everyone says that. It is too weak to tempt a new customer to pick up the phone and call you. There is no difference between this company and all the others standing on your doorstep with their hands out.

How to develop a Unique Selling Proposition (USP)

This takes a little uninterrupted time with your key employees. What you are looking for is the purpose of the company, expressed in a short and lively way.

Step One: If you have a motto or repetitive way of describing the company, write it down.

Then consider, if you are the founder of this company, why you went into this business in the first place. Did you see a market opening? Was the competition a terrible underperformer? In what specific ways that you can measure did you plan to offer a better product or service?

Then pull out the Yellow Pages and take a long hard look at your competitors. Do their advertisements grab you? What words and what services do they offer that would benefit the customer?

Go to the library and borrow a New York or Los Angeles Yellow Pages book and do the same analysis. If the books are not available any longer, then try the Internet. List the services and benefits they offer.

Then, list the features of your product and how they benefit your customer. List them all and then cross off any that your customer cannot measure. For example, "fair prices" is not a measurable benefit to the customer. On the other hand, "open Saturdays" is.

When developing your Unique Selling Proposition, view your product or service from your customer's position. Look from the point of view of someone thinking about buying from your company. Why should he or she buy from you? What is important to your potential customer? What would be a compelling reason to choose your company instead of the competition?

Remember that customers are only motivated by benefits, not features. Benefits are all about how your product adds value, while features relate to what goes into making the product or service and how it is made available to customers. Features are things like heavy duty springs, but the benefit — the thing that customers are buying — is reliability and durability. This is an important distinction.

Now you have a short list of benefits from which to choose. To decide which one is the most suitable as the focus of your Unique Selling Proposition, ask yourself these questions. Which benefits are likely the most important to your client? Which are your salespeople telling you are the most important? Which benefits are the most difficult for your competitors to imitate and therefore make your product or service unique? If your benefit is difficult to imitate, it will be difficult for them to follow. Which benefits can be most easily understood by customers? Is the best benefit so convoluted you need a Ph.D. in astrophysics to understand? Can you express this benefit in down-to-earth words?

Then list all the benefits and features your competitors advertise. Cross off those that are common to you and your competitors. If you cross off all of them, then you have more work to do to find something that is truly unique.

Finally, describe your ideal customer. Where does he or she live? What income level or what lifestyle? What problem are you solving for your customer?

TABLE 10
USP WORKSHEET

	Me	Them
Company Motto		
What the Company Set Out to Do from Day 1		
How the Competition Describes Their Service		
New York and Los Angeles Providers		
How Your Service Benefits the Customer		
Describe the Customer (the demographics)		

You will probably end up with several pages of notes. When you have identified the benefits you want to use, you can start writing the USP. Start off with a paragraph that describes the unique benefit or package of benefits. Then eliminate all unnecessary words.

Cut it down until you have only one sentence, 25 words or less, that says it all. Replace all flabby, general words with words that electrify and create a mental picture.

Does your company already have a Unique Selling Proposition? In years of business consulting, I have asked that question many times and been told by the owner that "we have the best prices in town" or "we have the best service in town." I would venture to offer that if this is your response then your company does not stand out in the crowd, and your company is not fulfilling its profit potential.

With a fully articulated USP, it is possible to command better prices. A fully articulated USP makes your company unique by emphasizing the differences that add value to the product or service. What benefit is the customer actually buying? Is it the convenience of being able to buy on Sunday? Is it that your warranty is four times longer than the competition? Is it that your counter staff are all ex-service technicians who understand how to fix things? Is it that your store is the only one in the mall with a playground for toddlers?

How can the small business owner apply this knowledge and turn it magically into cash? Consider one widget or job that your company offers. What was the original concept in selling it? Was it because no one offered this product or service? Or that they offered it badly? If you have competition, what makes your product or service better than the others?

What makes your company different? Are you just one of many? Have you been servicing the local market since 1899? Do you demonstrate reliability and longevity?

Do your servicemen vacuum when they're done the job?

Do you have the only "trendy" color scheme in town or the fastest snowmobiles?

What makes your business unique and does it fit the above criteria? If all you can offer is "we have better service" then you are in the commodity pricing market. However, even in the so–called commodity markets where price is supposed to be the only determinant, a Unique Selling Proposition differentiates the providers. "Consider the pragmatism of the Detroit auto manufacturers in buying sheet steel to exceedingly tight technical specifications, but it specifies much more than the steel itself. It also demands certain delivery conditions and flexibilities, price and payment conditions, and reordering responsiveness. From year to year, the Detroit companies shift the proportions of steel they buy from their various suppliers on the basis of elaborate grading systems that measure each supplier's performance on the specified conditions, including the kind and quality of unsolicited help on such matters as new materials ideas, ides for parts redesign, and even purchasing procedures."[11]

If you are offering the same product as everyone else — snowmobiles from Yamaha, software from Microsoft or roofing tiles from DuPont — you can still find ways to differentiate the way the company delivers the goods. Do you offer what the competition cannot offer? Do you offer service in the home? Or on Saturdays?

Example: Bugs Burger Bug Killer Company [12]

Why force people to pay for things that they don't value in the end? The Bugs Burger Bug Killer Company, based in Miami,

---

11. Theodore Leavitt. "Marketing success through differentiation — of anything." Harvard Business Review. January-February 1980.
12. Christopher W. L. Hart. Extraordinary Guarantees: Achieving Breakthrough Gains in quality and Customer Satisfaction.

Florida and run by Al Burger, is a pest control company specializing in the hospitality industry. Mr. Burger knew most companies did not want to control pests, but to wipe them out, so he developed an extraordinary guarantee to ensure his customers he could do the job.

The guarantee ran something like this: "You don't owe me one cent until all pests on your premises have been completely eradicated. If your guest spots a pest on the premises our company will pay for your guest's meal or room, send a letter of apology, and pay for a future meal or stay.

If you are ever dissatisfied with the company's service, you will receive a full refund of the company's services plus fees for another exterminator of your choice for the next year.

If your facility is closed down due to the presence of roaches or rodents, the company will pay any fines, as well as any lost profits, plus $5,000."

This extraordinary guarantee made this company stand head and shoulders above its nearest competition.

How about this promise from H&R Block that adds value and commands the price by reducing risk:

"We Take Responsibility for Our Mistakes

Our associate training and system of safeguards are carefully designed to ensure the accuracy of your return. Mistakes are rare at H&R Block. However, if we do make an error in the preparation of your tax return that costs you any interest or penalty on additional taxes due, we will reimburse you for the interest and penalty."[13]

What makes you and your company so different that you can justify more dollars? If you were a customer of either of the above companies, wouldn't it make sense to pay their top dollar? Even better, the above guarantee forces the customer to focus on the value proposition of a low-end service provider. Being shut down is a fear of most managers of hotels and restaurants. The costs and damage to reputation would be astronomical. So the cost of roach control is minor compared to that, right? Why buy cheap for such a critical service? And being called upon by the Internal Revenue Service or Canada Revenue Agency is a nightmare most of us would

---

13. http://www.hrblock.ca/our_company/guarantee.asp

pay money to avoid. So why not use the services of H&R Block with their great guarantee?

TABLE 11
FAB EXAMPLES

FEATURE	ADVANTAGE	BENEFIT
You have 10,000 line items in inventory	You are likely to have items in stock when customers need them	Speed of purchase
You only use non-allergenic cleaning products	Fewer clients will get sick because of chemicals	The customer will have fewer sick days being used
The company was formed in 1989	Customers know you are not a fly-by-night company	The customer is more likely to feel they have made a good buying decision

If the feature of a janitorial company is the use of non-allergenic cleaning products then the advantage is that fewer clients will get sick because of the chemicals used in the cleaning which will mean that the customer will pay for fewer sick days as his or her employees are less likely to become ill.

If the feature of the company is that it was formed in 1989 then the advantage is that they are not fly-by-night, so the customer is more likely to feel they have made a good buying decision.

Often enough the biggest problem facing a re-examination of price structure is that the company has become comfortable in its groove of selling an item at 49 cents when in fact there is a chance that they could sell the same quantity for $3.49.

You leave money on the table when you don't know what your customer wants and what he or she is prepared to pay for the value you add to your product or service.

EXAMPLE

Suppose that your supplier offers a sale on a fast-moving item. By merely passing along the price discount, you are not building your business. But if you got a 10 percent discount from your supplier, then the tenth case is free to you. That free case can be used to "buy" a difficult customer.

Promoting a sale is standard business practice. Some people drop prices to lure in customers who come to look and then buy something else. This gets customers familiar with the store or business, is an inexpensive way to get new products seen, and creates a little buzz.

TABLE 12
PROMOTIONAL PRICING

	Phase 1	Phase 2	Phase 3
2x4 Wall Studs	Heavy promotion	No promotion	Special price to trade only
Nails	Competition with buyers	Free nails as samples	No promotion
Glue	Discounts for display	Free glue with every gallon of paint	New product launch
Paint	No promotion	On-pack discount with orders of glue	Buy 2 get 1 free

The above table is one way to look at applying the concepts of promotional discount pricing. It provides a guideline on spending, knitting together product lines, a surprise to keep everyone interested, and a rational order for a successful promotion.

Years ago when I owned a hardware store, my friend and I were discussing the myopia of our respective customer bases. It was amusing and disconcerting to us that customers knew the price of perhaps ten items intimately. They knew where the best prices were to be had and when sales happened. For a supplier they were a nightmare because they expected us to meet or improve upon those prices. But to drop the price to meet the expectations of one client meant dropping that price for everyone, using standard inventory-control software. Worse, there would be an impact upon the bottom line since the ten items Fred remembered were neither the same ten items recalled by Joe nor the same ten as memorized by Richard. Maintaining some sort of handy list to remind us and our staff that a special price was available for chosen clients, and then overriding the standard pricing was a clumsy remedy. We tried that.

Ultimately, I hit on some software that would allow me to adjust prices for one customer but not another, thereby mainlining the profit margins.

But the real point of the discussion was how a customer, client, or patient feels about your overall pricing based upon just a few scraps of information. This is where the promotional pricing ideas in Table 12 work well to create an impression of features, advantages, and benefits without really dropping prices to dangerous levels.

All of us monitor the price of gasoline, and we have all seen in person or on TV the long lineups of cars trying to get gas before it jumps one cent. Yet we happily pay more for bottled water than for gasoline. So paying attention to what your customers are telling you in discussion or through their buying practices is the route to profit Nirvana. You can be viewed as the best buy on the street or the one to avoid because you gouge people. Your choice.

What clear benefit does your company offer to your customers — a benefit so obvious that price is not a part of the sales discussion?

Odd things that happen with pricing

Studies of consumer markets show that discounts of less than 10 percent elicit hardly any customer response. Offers of between 10 percent and 12 percent exhibited a correlation between discount and sales in over half the cases recorded. Discounts in excess of 13 percent are distinctly linked to increased sales. But the larger the discount, the less likely it is that the brand will maintain its increased share of the market afterwards.

Many studies in diverse parts of the world show that high price is associated in the consumer's mind with high quality. This holds especially true where fashion or taste is concerned. Why else would perfumes and champagne sell for such astronomical prices?

Franchises

This is the point of franchises. The benefit of a McDonald's restaurant is that the Big Mac will taste the same whether you bought it in Tokyo, Toronto, or Berlin. The price may vary from country to country, but the delivered product does not. Coca-Cola has the same idea.

For some franchises the price is the benefit and is used to set the company apart from the competition. The niche market franchisors like Mr. Lube have created a business out of having a one price shop. Are there cheaper places to get an oil change? Undoubtedly, but they do not have the marketing and advertising clout to carve out a large share of the available market.

When I owned an installation company in Vancouver in the 1980s and 1990s, we struggled hard to keep prices universal for standard jobs. Our marketing edge — successfully employed to gain an 80 percent market share — was to offer the benefit of a fixed price where none had existed before. Customers bought our services because we gave them a closed-ended transaction.

Perceived Value

Most customers have an inherent notion of what things should cost. These notions may be based upon solid research on the Internet, phoning for dozens of quotes, or just chatting with family and friends.

However, for some items, the cost bears no relationship to the price. This is particularly true where the benefits have elbowed price off the table.

For some years there was a mighty battle between Intel and AMD to dominate the market for processing chips. Intel kept ahead of its competition by being innovative and adding features faster than its competitors. Its Pentium chip took a huge market share until AMD invested heavily and matched the Pentium's performance. That eliminated Intel's pricing advantage. "Recognizing that AMD could quickly match future technological advances made by Intel, management turned their attention from features that drove customer costs and were easy to copy, to features that drove customer revenues and were harder to copy."[14]

Their research showed that customers were more likely to buy a product when they knew what processor was in the box. Hence was born the "Intel Inside" marketing campaign. Intel commanded a premium price for the chip because its advertising drove the sales of the computer manufacturers. AMD could not follow since it was lesser known, except among computer geeks.

Who Is Your Customer?

Finding the right price for the right customer is a constant challenge for every business whether it sells wedding plans, concrete patios, books, installations, or repair services.

For any product, a business must understand its positioning before it can set a price.

---

14. *Strategy and Tactics of Pricing: Guide to Grow More Profitably 4th ed, 2006.* Nagle, T.E. and Hogan, E. H. Pearson. Reprinted by permission of Pearson Education, Inc., Upper Saddle River, NJ.

If the business targets the wealthy, where price is no object, then sale prices make no sense. Money is the tool to acquire benefits and features. When targeting the wealthy, your product or service has to be exclusive or at least be seen to be exclusive. Is your company the Mercedes-Benz of your industry?

If your business targets seniors, then price might be 100 percent of the buying decision.

EXAMPLE

Sometimes knowing your market leads to unexpected decisions. In the 1980s we marketed our installation company's services to the supposedly well-to-do part of town. We got the calls and did the work, only to be told that the check would be in the mail or have credit cards rejected. The service technicians told me tales of installing top-of-the-line products in houses where the furniture was upturned plastic milk crates.

At the same time, our business in the "working class" part of Vancouver produced no problems. In fact, most often we were paid in cash from a roll of bills from the pocket of the homeowner.

The lesson: Part of your target market consideration should be the ability to pay.

So What, You Say?

Imagine that today you have $50,000 in your pocket and you want to buy a luxury car. The salesperson keeps showing you economy cars. Will you buy? Is it price that makes the decision for you?

Or, imagine that today you need a car to get you back and forth from work. You have $15,000 and on the lot is a General Motors product for the $15,000 and beside it is a $475 car made by some company you have never heard of before.

Compare food the same way. A higher price is usually charged for Heinz ketchup than for generic brands.

Make sure your price is not too low, or customers will not put great value on your product or service. If it is too high, customers will not take the risk.

Think Like a Customer

"On the principle that effective product pricing must be based on customer economics, successful industrial marketers, when calculating how much financial incentive their prices should reflect, give careful consideration to the cost and the risk the customer may incur in purchasing their products.... Some successful marketers routinely apply this kind of analysis before they make any major commitment to a new industrial product."[15]

What this means is that in trying to convert a potential customer to your line of floor wax stripper, you must first find out his or her hidden costs. In converting will he or she have to retrain staff? In converting will he or she have to retrain his or her customers? What will he or she do with the 450 gallons of the stripper currently in the warehouse? Will he or she have to update the sales brochures?

Step One: Analyze your customer

Once you have the USP and the FAB and can, in 25 words or less, articulate these differences, it is time to apply the same thinking to your customers. Who in your customer list will respond best to these arguments and will accept price increases? Who, in the untouched marketplace, will respond positively to being told that your product or service will save them untold thousands in reduced downtime?

The cost of your product or service is evaluated by a purchaser in terms of the functionality of the offering, the costs, the durability, the reliability, the after market service, freight, installation, and payment terms.

In your sales offering, have you addressed each of these in a way that means something to the customer? If not, price will become the determining factor.

A study published in 1954 illustrates the outcome of this "value-pricing" process.

"In July, 1954, DuPont introduced Alathon 25, a new polyethylene resin used in pipe manufacture. Until that time, all polyethylene pipes had been made from a by-product of off-grade resin. While pipe produced from Alathon 25 looked exactly like pipe made from off-grade resin, it had a longer life than competitive pipe and could withstand greater pressure.

---

15. Elliot B. Ross. "Making Money with Proactive Pricing." Harvard Business Review. N0. 84614. November-December 1984.

After the product's shaky entry in to the market, DuPont developed a strong promotional program for Alathon 25 which communicated its notable benefits to a careful selection of the extruders who made the resin into pipe. Alathon 25 sales grew strongly despite the fact that extruders sold the pipe to distributors for between $9.50 and $13.00 per 100 feet versus the $5.00 to $7.00 price for pipe made from off-grade resin. This price ratio, almost 1.9 is greater than the relative lives of the pipe would suggest.

An advertisement reproduced in the case study shows the secret of this strategy's success. It shows a farm application, a typical use of this pipe, were the pipe goes underground. It is clear that if the pipe bursts, it would have to be dug up — a time consuming and expensive chore. The value or utility of the pipe is great because it is part of a complex system."[16]

Step Two: Market benefits, not features

Unless your customer is an engineer, the latest precut specifications are gibberish. Your new resin, new alloy, or new gadget must answer the WIFM (What's in it for me?) question if it is to be sold. The above example clearly demonstrates the transition. Alathon 25 would burst but at greater pressures. The benefit to the end user was the savings in not digging up burst pipe as often. At that point price became irrelevant.

In another example, it could be new drill bits with titanium points. They are harder and can drill longer without sharpening. But that has to become a tangible benefit by translating from longer between sharpenings to 14 percent more holes drilled. At that point, the potential bulk user might whip out a calculator and cost out his or her downtime for drill changes and then the cost of re-sharpening. Price has become a secondary issue.

Step Three: Examine the cost variables

Before setting price levels, examine the customer perception of what a cost is.

Look at restructuring your business to identify costs you need not swallow which are driving your prices. Can you successfully extract and "unbundle" your product and service, terms of payment, terms of delivery and shipment, turnaround time, warranties, and

---

16. Benson P. Shapiro and Barbara B. Jackson. "Industrial Pricing to meet customer needs." Harvard Business Review. No.78609. November-December 1978.

after-sales technical help? If so, will that help sales by being able to offer the same product without changing your prices, and can the extras be sold as add-ons?

"One manufacturer of laboratory instruments was plagued by a high number of very small orders for a limited variety of repair parts for one particular product line. On analysis, the product manager found that customers were annoyed at having to order small parts because the ordering cost was greater than the parts prices. Furthermore, the company was losing money on the parts for that same reason.

Even more costly, customers were upset at the downtime caused by not having the correct parts in stock. A few customers with many instruments seemed capable of keeping the right mix of parts in stock but others with limited experience could not develop good inventory rules. To alleviate the problem, the product manager developed repair kits with several different assortments of parts and offered them to customers using a large variety of instruments. The company's costs went down, customer costs decreased, and customer satisfaction increased because instruments were available more of the time."[17]

This example lends itself well to building a case before price is mentioned in the sales presentation. Downtime is a cost in the eyes of the customer.

Now that you understood the basics of value, it is time to go forth and examine in detail the value proposition and how it can be used to determine pricing structures.

Summary

Your company needs a Unique Selling Proposition in order to find value in the products and services you offer to your customer. Without this key piece of business understanding, whatever you sell will be a commodity in the eyes of the customer, and you will be undifferentiated from your competition across town.

In this chapter I have outlined the steps to create a USP. Carefully translate that USP into a marketing proposition showing Features, Advantages and Benefits to the customer. Then examine your customer list for people who will not accept your arguments and those who will. Those who will not accept your arguments need a

---

17. Benson P. Shapiro and Barbara B. Jackson. "Industrial Pricing to meet customer needs." Harvard Business Review. No.78609.

better reason to buy from you. Finally, a truthful look at your costs will give you the foundation from which to polish your USP, FAB, and marketing program.

Then you can proceed with confidence into learning the techniques of value-driven pricing in the next chapter.

5
VALUE-DRIVEN PRICING

Pricing Down from Value versus Pricing Up from Cost

Value, like truth, beauty, and contact lenses, is in the eye of the beholder.

Value, to a purchaser of fashion, is less about clothes than it is about looking attractive, stylish, and self-confident. The price of fashion, therefore, is not driven purely by cost, but also by value.

Consider the price of fish. Is the price of fish driven by costs? If a fisherman hauls in a net full of salmon you could assign costs for all the labor involved in laying out the nets and hauling them back in and then processing the fish. Add to that the cost of the boat, fuel, and depreciation, and you are well on your way to a standard accountant-driven cost-pricing structure.

But what happens if a fish accidentally jumps into the boat? Is there no cost attached to that fish? If so, then does that fish have no price?

The purpose of this chapter is to demonstrate the incredible success of value pricing. But where do costs fit in? Creating prices by marking up from cost is complicated enough. But it also leaves money on the table because this approach pretends to know better than the customer the value of the item or service purchased.

Although still in its infancy, the value-driven model for pricing has, in the past ten years, become the focus of interest for innumerable scholarly articles. Although the reader may complain legitimately that I have not given them enough practical tools to use this approach every day, this is because these tools are still being developed. I believe that the effort to make it apply to your business will reward you with greater and greater profits by leaving less money on the table than your competitors leave, by keeping you focused on what your company can do for your customer and keeping your company trim and nimble.

Let us consider the lesson to be learned from Ford and General Motors first to illustrate the hazards of cost-up pricing and the benefits of price-down costing. In the 1950s, when General Motors decided to build a sports car to compete with the European sports cars that were entering the market, the brass went to the engineering department first. The engineers were told to design a sports car. They did and produced a vehicle based on some common GM platforms like the Belair frame but with added refinements for appearances and performance. They built an engineer's car! At the end of the process, the costs were put on the table and a factor added for profit and presto, there was the sale price at $3,450. It didn't sell well because it was considered too expensive. At one point the Corvette sold a mere 700 units in a year and was saved from the axe by some enthusiastic and devoted engineers.

In 1960 or thereabouts, Ford also conceived the idea of having a sports car. Lee Iacocca, previous Ford president, went first to the marketing department and asked them where the price needed to be in order to sell lots of cars. The research engine got into gear and cranked out $2,500. Iacocca then took this number to engineering and gave them a list of specifications that included the price tag. They fought back about getting the costs that low but ultimately, 2 inches longer, 200 pounds heavier, built on a Falcon frame, festooned with common Ford components and eight months behind schedule, they produced a car for a selling price of $2,500. The Mustang sold its millionth car after just 13 months and is still highly regarded as a marketing success story.

Next we will examine some common industries and how you can find the value a customer attaches to your product or service.

Contracting: A Recommended Strategy for Finding the Customer's Buying Price

Top-down selling is the approach whereby, after creating your Unique Selling Proposition, you start with a high level assessment of the customer requirements. Add all the bells and whistles and price them out at your best (highest) price. Present the estimate personally. If you present this price over the phone or in the mail, you will not be able to respond to the emotional reaction if the response is anything but "Okay, go ahead." If the customer appears deflated or shocked, then rewrite the bid by first asking what he or she thought it might cost. Now you have two things. You have the customer's budget and the upper limit of the customer's expectations. Rewrite the bid so that it subtracts some non-essential items or substitutes cheaper replacements.

Retailing: Testing the Water

I believe that in retail the key to success is trial and error. After you have developed a Unique Selling Proposition for the company and have trained your sales staff to offer world class service, and you have sufficient product knowledge for the sales staff to paint a glowing picture of the product and why the customer should buy this particular item, then you can tinker with the prices. If an item sells moderately well at $4.99, can you re-price it at $6.99 and maintain the sales? Putting up the price does not always mean that the sales will go down. In some instances, the price is an indication of quality. Selling cheap means a substandard product in some customers' eyes. Do Rolex watches cost so much more to manufacture than Timex watches? Is the price driven by cost or the distinction of having a premium watch to brag about?

Of course, tracking sales is the key to this approach. You will have to know definitively that the sales have increased over a measurable period. And if sales went down, you may wish to interview a few people or check your competition.

The impact is that prices in a retail store must move about constantly to find the right level. When you have reached the right price level and sales have stabilized you have found the value price. Now you attack the cost structure.

Some items, are not price sensitive. For essential items — are you a destination store or a store needing high volumes of traffic? — people will search for your store. For bigger ticket items they will perhaps shop by telephone. For smaller items, they will ask, "Do you have it on the shelf?"

Some items are just price insensitive and the customer will not buy more at any lower price, nor will they balk at higher prices if the need is urgent. Consider the December 24th buying frenzy in any shopping mall in the country.

My favourite story about price insensitivity is actually reserved for advertising but works well here. In my Richmond-based hardware store, I frequently had young, inexperienced salespeople come to the store to sell me newspaper advertising. I remember a conversation that went like this:

Salesperson:	"Of course, you will sell more if you advertise."
Me:	"And what should I advertise?"
Salesperson:	"Well, advertise a sale and customers will hammer at the doors."
Me:	"Well, you see these 60 bake elements hanging over your head?"
Salesperson (now sensing a trap):	"Yes ... "
Me:	"Well the regular retail price is $30. For the next 10 minutes they are $10 apiece. How many would you like to take home with you?"
Salesperson:	"Well, I don't really need one, never mind several."
Me (triumphant):	"So you see the point; that we are a destination store and unless you need a bake element you will not buy one at any time at any price. Therefore, I would be wasting my money on the advertising you suggest."

And what about stores that offer benefits aside from a great product at a value price? Donald Cooper described how customers drove a hundred miles to visit his clothing store in Guelph, Ontario, because he catered to the emotional needs of the women who shopped there. He used part of the valuable space of his store to offer a space for women with children after noting that women accompanied by children would have fewer than ten minutes of time to shop for the right skirt or blouse before the children got bored and demanded to go home. The play area solved that because the children were occupied and safe and the mothers could shop for as long as they wished. To those shoppers, the clothing on the racks was cheap at any price, since Cooper gave them free, quiet, personal time.

EXAMPLE

A florist shop was having trouble balancing the artistic instincts of its flower arrangers with the requirements for consistency and cost. Some $100 bouquets were staggeringly beautiful constructions studded with expensive tropical flowers and cost much more than the $100 price tag. The florists would also make some hasty arrangements created from inexpensive flowers also priced at $100. The lack of consistency sent a message to customers receiving the tired arrangements that their business was unwelcome. Trouble ensued, of course.

To achieve consistency, the solution was to start with the price tag, say $50, and work backwards. All prices of the components include landed cost plus a factor for wastage and profit.

TABLE 13
FLORIST EXAMPLE

Items	Cost per unit	Quantity	Extended	Running
Opening price				$50.00
Roses	$4.00	4	$16.00	$34.00
Calla lilies	$8.00	2	$16.00	$18.00
Curly hazel	$0.45	8	$3.60	$14.40
12" medium glass vase	$3.95	1	$3.95	$10.45
Ribbon	$1.00	4 feet	$4.00	$6.45
Card	$1.00	1	$1.00	$5.45
Oasis	$0.35	2	$0.70	$4.75
One last rose	$4.00	1	$4.00	$0.75

In the example, the running totals helped the florists know how much to add or subtract from their orders. Each bucket of water containing the roses and the lilies was clearly labeled with a large price tag. The florists could feel free with their artistic whims yet, working backwards, still achieve a profitable sale.

Why did this work? Because the customer came into the store with only two expectations: Beauty and the limits of his or her wallet. So the store began the sales process with the final price and showed some examples in the customer's price range. In this florist shop the sales effort became directed at managing customer expectations while achieving a more consistent product. Before, the customer was shown sample bouquets and more or less asked what flowers he or she wanted, but now the transaction became price- and value-driven.

The failure of this approach is that money is left on the table. It does keep costs under control — that is precisely what this business needed most at that time. However, in the end it is the perceived value of the offering that determines the price. After all, does anyone care how long it takes for GM to build a car?

Consulting

A decade ago, I worked for a Chicago-based business consultancy. My first exposure to value-based pricing occurred in training and I did not, at the time, realize what was happening. Most of the focus of the training period was on gaining familiarity with the tools to analyze a business and pick apart areas of cost and deviations from the norm. So far, that is standard cost accounting methodology.

Then we practiced adding together the costs over a period of years and presenting this as the opportunity cost if the business was as well-managed as it could be. This, we all knew, was a sales technique: Telling people how much money they could save.

Then we came to the question of the fees that would be charged for a program to rectify this situation. At this point, none of the trainers gave a straight answer. "What would you like it to be?" was the response. We were all dumbfounded and spent a few hours in the bar afterwards discussing this cryptic answer. How, after all, could we place a number on the value of a consulting contract from knowing only the financial penalties being paid for not correcting the business?

But that is precisely what was required. If the costs over a period of 4 years had been $180,000 then a fair price could be anywhere from $180,000 (1:1 and a little unlikely) to $1 (1: 180,000, also unrealistic). Since my pay was derived as a percentage of the contracts I sold, the price trended upwards. After a few years I started to pay attention to the client's cash flow so that the check would be easy to write.

So the moral of the story is to know exactly what the customer's penalty is for not proceeding with the consultancy contract and creating a fee structure that is a fraction of those costs. Of course, you must know the time you expect to spend on this project and the out-of-pocket expenses you will probably incur. Likely, a successful consultant already goes through this process. If the selling price is higher than your expected costs, then you have a profit.

Ronald Baker's book[18] quotes at length an early attempt at value pricing that was a huge success and convinced an accounting company to abandon hourly rates and go to TIP pricing. A TIP clause in contracts is also referred to as a retrospective price clause or success pricing. Example of this type of clause: In the event that we are able to satisfy your needs in a timely and professional manner, you have agreed to review the situation and decide whether, at the sole discretion of XYZ Company, some additional payment to ABC, the consultant, is appropriate in view of your overall satisfaction with the services rendered by ABC.

Apparently the story begins in Las Vegas at a conference where Mr. Baker met a friend, a partner in an accounting firm. The friend then spent some time relating his amazing TIP story. The two e-mails he received from this friend to explain his success are summarized below.

Email One:

The firm was in the middle of a $180,000 contract that had started a month or two before, quoted using the old standard rate-times-hours routine at a standard rate of $180/hour.

The owner revisited his clients to explain that he felt, after due consideration, that the price needed revisiting. He told the client that the work they were undertaking would undoubtedly produce a high value return and that only the client could set a true value the

18. Baker. Ronald J. Pricing on Purpose. Creating and Capturing Value. John Wiley and Sons Inc. Hoboken, New Jersey. 2006 p 115-6.

service being offered. He threw his accounting firm at the mercy of the client, who would have been truly shocked.

Email Two:

This email explained the final result after the job was done. The friend related how he had used a flip chart presentation explaining the value of what they were getting. At the end of the presentation, he asked what they thought this might be worth and suggested $300,000 or even $500,000 in order to get them to think in big numbers. The CEO got rather excited and said a million.

It got even better because he knew that getting one check for $1 million would be tough so he suggested a retainer of $400,000 and then monthly payments. The clients agreed and asked GS to serve on the board of directors and attend quarterly meetings until the note to the previous owners was paid off. This all adds up to a little bit over $1 million. As the friend related to Mr. Baker, never once was the word "time" used. The client couldn't have cared less about time.

In all future engagements, he never used the word. Instead, by concentrating on value and encouraging the client to participate in the valuation of the engagement, the accounting firm's revenue and prices skyrocketed.

Service Businesses

Typically in service businesses, customers ask for prices because you are selling someone else's labor and that is easy to compare. Here, your company's Unique Selling Proposition comes directly into play.

First mention what sets you apart from the competition. Then, list all the bells and whistles your company offers before you get to price. If possible, never quote an hourly rate. Bundle services together in price bands that can satisfy your market.

After giving the price, if the customer appears deflated or shocked, then ask what he or she thought it might cost. Now you have two things. You have the customer budget and the upper limit of the customer's expectations. Rewrite the bid so that it subtracts some non-essential items or substitutes for cheaper replacements.

Selling Industrially or Working with a Professional Buyer

This entails homework beforehand. A little research can yield whether or not the customer is genuine or just shopping around. Or are you prepared to create detailed Requests for Quotes (RFQs) on demand for any potential buyer?

Ask questions such as "What happened to your last supplier?" The answer may show they are unreasonable, picky, or a customer that sees value. Pay attention to the complaints about past providers. These are definitely the value indicators that you will need to have in your package for you to succeed.

Ask what importance your product plays in the buyer's business. If you are the coffee supplier and the buyer's life was made miserable from all the complaints about the coffee last year, the coffee is important.

Do the customers pay on time? Do they argue on the final payout? Do they reject large percentages of product for fictitious reasons? The answers will affect your price.

Are they reasonable about delivery times or detailed about the day and time? Do they expect penalty clauses for late deliveries?

Finally, after you have done all this homework, are you dealing with the person who makes the final decisions? Suppose you have spent several weeks cultivating a relationship with that buyer, produced a detailed RFQ only to have it pass out of the "buyer's" hands to the company's buying committee who have never met you and know nothing about you or your company except the price typed on your RFQ.

Ultimately, the best advice possible would be to try out prices on the buyer first before committing to a detailed RFQ. After all, if your $1,100 widget with a four-year warranty causes the buyer go into shock, then perhaps a $975 widget with a single year warranty is more palatable. Would it not be easier and safer to see an informal reaction to your offer before committing it to paper?

Distributing

Price, for a distributor, is not the only factor in determining a sale. Sometimes it is purely availability. If you have the o-ring that I need to repair the bulldozer sitting idle instead of being used to build a road, then any price for an o-ring is reasonable. You will have my thanks just for having the part.

But other parts of the selling package are credit terms, delivery, and minimum order.

And then there are the intangibles, such as how difficult it is for me to park my vehicle in your parking lot and whether the staff are knowledgeable and get me the right part the first time, and quickly.

The key element in determining your price level will be listening to the customer. Customers are sensitive to only a handful of prices. If you know what those prices are then you can make up the lost profits on those items about which they are clueless.

And if Bob finds out that his repair kit is costing him more than Fred's repair kit? You can simply say "Well, Bob, Fred has a special price because he buys 100 a month. I can help you if you want to buy 100 a month too."

Customer Behavior and Perceived Value

A study by Nagle and Hogan on pricing in their book *"The Strategy and Tactics of Pricing: A Guide to Growing More Profitably"* contains this gem of an exposition on customer behavior and perceived value. I have mentioned it here because it demonstrates the depth of the research, scholarship and understanding of the problems of running a business.

Price communication

Although it is easy to understand how value can be influenced, particularly the perceived value of psychological benefits, prices would seem to be hard data that are relatively easy to compare and communicate. But research over the years has repeatedly shown that people do not necessarily evaluate prices logically. Customers can perceive the same price paid in return for the same value differently depending on how it is communicated. Let's examine four aspects of price perception and their implications on price communication: proportional price evaluations, reference prices, perceived fairness, and gain-loss framing.

Proportional price evaluations

Buyers tend to evaluate price differences proportionally rather than in absolute terms. For example, one research study asked customers if they would leave a store and go to one nearby to save $5 on a purchase. Of respondents who were told that the price in the first store was $15, some 68 percent said they would go to the other store to buy the product for $10. Of respondents who were told that the price in the first store was $125, only 29 percent would switch stores to buy the product for $120. Similar studies have replicated this effect, including research with business manager respondents. When the $5 difference was proportionally — 33 percent of the lower price — it was more motivating than when it was proportionally a small part, 4 percent of the higher price.

Psychologists call the tendency to evaluate price differences proportionately the Weber-Fechner effect. It has clear implications for price communication. For example, auto companies increased the motivational power of their rebate promotions when they offered the option of free financing instead of a fixed-dollar rebate only. Despite the fact that the present value of the interest saved was no more, and often less, than the value of the fixed-dollar rebate, free financing proved more popular. Why? Because eliminating 100 percent of the financing cost motivated consumers more than a 5 percent discount on a $20,000 car. Similarly, hotel chains have found it more effective to offer free breakfast or free Internet access with their rooms rather than offer a slightly lower price.

An important implication of Weber-Fechner is that price change perceptions depend on the percentage, not the absolute difference, and that there are thresholds above and below a product's price at which price changes are noticed or ignored. A series of smaller price increases below the upper threshold is more successful than one large increase. Conversely, buyers respond more to one large price cut below the lower threshold than to a series of smaller, successive discounts. For example, one full-service brokerage house raised its commissions every six months over a three-year period with little resistance from customers. Seeing this success, its competitor tried to match these increases in one large step and received intense criticism.

Reference Prices

Economists and market researchers generally focus on the trade-off that buyers make between the utility they get from the product or service and the price they pay. One key element in this research is called transaction utility theory, which suggests that buyers are motivated by more than just the utility associated with obtaining and using a product. The transaction utility also motivates buyers. That is the difference between the price actually paid and what the buyer considers a reasonable or fair reference price for the product.

We explored the role of competitive prices in pegging what buyers consider the reference price. Other types of information also influence the reference price, information sellers can manage to their advantage.

A common approach relies on careful product line pricing, as illustrated in Table 14. A controlled experiment asked subjects to choose among different models of microwave ovens. Researchers asked half the subjects to choose between two models (Emerson and Panasonic); the other half chose from among three models (Emerson, Panasonic I, and Panasonic II). Although 13 percent of the subjects were drawn to the top-end model, the Panasonic II, the largest impact of adding that third-model choice was on the Panasonic I, which gained 17 additional share points when it became the mid-priced choice. The implications of product line pricing are clear. Adding a premium product to the product line may not necessarily result in overwhelming sales of the premium product itself. It does, however enhance buyers' perceptions of lower-priced products in the product line and encourages low-end buyers to trade up to higher-priced models.

TABLE 14
REFERENCE PRICES

Exhibit 5-7 Reference Price Effects on a High End Product.		
	Choice (percent)	
Microwave Oven Model	Group 1 (n = 60)	Group 2 (n=60)
Panasonic II (1.1 cubic feet; regular price $199.99; sale price 10 percent off)	0	13
Panasonic I (0.8 cubic feet; regular price $179.99; sale price 35 percent off)	43	60
Emerson (0.5 cubic feet; regular price $109.99; sale price 35 percent off)	57	27

Source: Itamar Simonson, and Amos Tversky, "Choice in Context: Tradeoff Contrast and Extremeness Aversion,"*Journal of Marketing Research,* 29 (August 1992).

Another way marketers can influence reference prices is by suggesting potential reference points. For example, buyers' reference prices can be raised by stating the manufacturer's suggested price, a higher price charged previously ("Was $999 … now $799!"), or a higher price charged by competitors ("Their price $999, Our price $799!"). Research indicates that advertisements suggesting reference prices are more effective in influencing consumer durable product purchases (video cameras) than ads that do not, particularly among less knowledgeable buyers who rely more on price to make buying decisions. Other studies have found that providing buyers with a suggested reference point enhances perceptions of value and savings, even if the advertised reference point is exaggerated. Although buyers may discount or question the credibility of such claims, the claims still favorably influence perceptions and behaviors.

The order of presentation evidently influences customers' reference prices. In seminal research on this effect, two groups of experimental subjects saw the same sets of prices for a number of products in eight product classes. One group saw the prices in descending order (from highest to lowest); the other group saw them in ascending order (from lowest to highest). Researchers then asked each subject how much the same individual product in each product class was priced "high" or "low" relative to its value. From those judgments, the researchers calculated average reference prices for each product. The result: Subjects who saw the prices in descending order formed higher reference prices than those who saw then in ascending order, even though both groups saw the same set of prices. When forming their reference prices, buyers apparently give greater weight to the prices they see first.

These results clearly have important implications for price communication. In personal selling, this reference price effect implies the salesperson should begin a presentation by first showing products above a customer's price range, even if the customer ultimately will choose from among cheaper products. This tactic, known as "top-down selling" is common for products as diverse as automobiles, luggage and real estate. Direct mail catalogues take advantage of this effect by displaying similar products in the order of most to least expensive. Within a retail store, the order effect has implications for product display. It implies, for example, that a grocery store might sell low-priced (but high margin) house brands by not putting them at eye level where they would be the first to catch the customer's attention. It may be preferable to have consumers see more expensive brands first and then look for the house brands.

Finally, promotional deals such as coupons, rebates, and special package sizes can influence reference prices strategically. Some marketers have argued that new precuts should be priced low to induce trial and thus build a market of repeat purchasers, after which price can be raised. But if the low initial price lowers buyers expectations it may actually affect repeat sales adversely. This is the result some researchers have found. In one well-controlled study, five new brands were introduced to the market in two sets of stores. During an introductory period, one set of stores sold the new brands at a low price without any indication that this was a temporary promotional price; the control stores sold the new brands at the regular price. As expected, the brands sold better during the introductory period where they were priced lower. During the weeks following the introduction, however, both sets of stores charged the regular price. In all five cases, sales during the post-introductory period were lower in the stores with the low initial price than control stores. Moreover, total sales for the introductory and post introductory periods combined were greater in the control stores than in the stores where low price initially stimulated demand. This and other studies showing similar results demonstrate the importance of discounting tactics. The seller should clearly establish a product's regular price and then promote the discount as a temporary price cut. Otherwise, initially low promotional prices designed to build product trial can establish low reference prices that will undermine the product's perceived value at regular prices later on.

Perceived Fairness

The concept of a "fair price" has bedeviled marketers for centuries. In the Middle Ages, merchants were put to death for exceeding public norms regarding the "just price." Even in modern market economies, "price gougers" often face press criticism, regulatory hassles, and public boycotts. Consequently, marketers should understand and attempt to manage perceptions of fairness. But what is fair? The concept of fairness appears to be totally unrelated to issues of supply and demand. Assumptions about the seller's profitability influence perceived fairness, but not entirely. Oil companies have often been accused of gouging, even when their profits are below average. When hurricane Katrina disrupted gasoline supplies in the American south, gas station owners who raised prices were soundly criticized as price gougers even though they had only enough supply to serve those who wanted the product at that price. In contrast to the situation faced by oil companies, popular forms of entertainment (Disney World, for example, or state lotteries) are very profitable and expensive, yet their pricing escapes widespread criticism.

Recent research seems to indicate that perceptions of fairness are more subjective, and therefore more manageable, than one might otherwise think. Buyers apparently start by comparing what they think is the seller's likely margin and what the seller earned in the past, or to what others earn in similar purchase contexts. In a famous experiment, people imagined that they were laying on the beach, thirsty for a favorite brand of beer, and that a friend was walking to a nearby location and would bring back beer if the price was not too high. Researchers asked them to specify the maximum amount that he or she would pay. Subjects did not know that half of them had been told that the friend would patronize a fancy resort hotel while the other half had been told that the friend would buy from a small grocery store. Although these individuals would not themselves visit or enjoy the amenities of the purchase location, the median acceptable price of those who expected the beer to come from the hotel — $2.65 — was dramatically higher than the median acceptable price given by those who expected it to come from the grocery store — $1.50.

Presumptions about the seller's motive influence customers' perceived fairness judgments. A seller justifying a higher price with a "good" motive (e.g., funding. employee health insurance, improving service levels) makes the price more acceptable than does a "bad" motive (e.g., exploiting a market shortage to increase stockholder profits). Research suggests that companies like Disney with good reputations are much more likely to get the benefit of the doubt about their motives. Those with unpopular reputations (e.g., oil companies) are likely to find their motives suspect.

Finally, perceptions of fairness seem to be related to whether the price is paid to maintain a standard of living, or is paid to improve a standard of living. People consider products that maintain a standard to be necessities, although humanity as probably survived without them for most of its history. Charging a high price for a necessity is generally considered unfair. For example, people object to prices for life-saving drugs because they feel that they shouldn't have to pay to be healthy. After all, they were healthy last year without having to buy prescriptions and medical advice. People react similarly to rent increases. Yet, the same individuals might buy a new car, jewelry, or a vacation without objecting to equally high prices or price increases

Fortunately, perceptions of fairness can be managed. Companies that frequently adjust prices to reflect supply and demand or to segment buyers with different price sensitivities are careful to set the regular price at the highest possible level, rather than at the average or most common price. This enables them to "discount" when necessary to move product at slow times (a "good" motive), rather than have to increase prices when demand is strong (a "bad" motive). Similarly, because buyers believe that companies should not have to lose money, it's often best to blame price increases on rising costs to serve customers. Buyers believe that is fair, such as when petroleum prices increase. Landlords who raise rents should announce property improvements at the same time. Innovative companies raise prices more successfully when they are launching a new product and say they are recovering development costs.

Gain-Loss Framing

A final consideration in price communication is presenting the price to customers, who tend to evaluate prices in terms of gains or losses from an expected price point. How they frame those judgments affects the attractiveness of the purchase. To illustrate this effect, grounded in prospect theory, ask yourself which of the following two gasoline stations you'd be more willing to patronize, assuming that you deem both brands to be equally good and you would always pay with a credit card.

- Station A sells gasoline for $2.20 per gallon, but gives a $0.20 per gallon discount if the buyer pays with cash.

- Station B sells gasoline for $2.00 per gallon, but charges a $0.20 per gallon surcharge if the buyer pays with a credit card.

Of course, the economic cost of buying gasoline from either station is identical. Yet, most people find the offer from station A more attractive than the offer from station B. The reason is that people place more psychological importance on avoiding losses than on capturing equal size gains. Also, both the gains and losses of an individual transaction are subject, independently, to diminishing returns, as one would expect from the Weber-Fechner effect we discussed earlier. A given change has less psychological impact the larger the base to which it is added or subtracted.

In our gas station example, cash buyers prefer A where they receive the psychological benefit of earning a discount, a "gain" to them. Paying the same $2.00 net price per gallon at station B, which offers no explicit discount, does not provide a psychological benefit.

Credit card buyers also prefer station A, mainly because station B's credit card surcharge creates a "loss," a negative psychological benefit to be avoided. Paying the same $2.20 net price per gallon at station A, which requires no explicit surcharge, does not provide a psychological benefit, positive or negative.

Buyers otherwise indifferent to paying by cash or credit will not be indifferent to stations A or B despite the sellers' economic value equivalence; such buyers would always pay cash to get the lowest price but would likely choose A to the psychological satisfaction unavailable at B.

Prospect theory has many implications for price communication:

- To make prices less objectionable, make them opportunity costs (gains forgone) rather than out-of-pocket costs. Banks often waive fees for checking accounts in return for maintaining a minimum balance. Even when the interest forgone on the funds in the account exceeds the charge for checking, most people choose the minimum balance option. People find it less painful to pay for things like insurance or mutual funds with payroll deductions instead of buying them outright.

- When your product is priced differently to different customers and at different times, set the list price at the highest level and give most people discounts. This type of pricing is so common that we take it for granted. Colleges, for example charge only a small portion of customers the list price and give everyone else discounts. To those who pay at or near the full price, the failure to receive more of a discount (a gain forgone) is much less objectionable than if they were asked to pay a premium because they are not star students, athletes, or good negotiators.

- Unbundle gains and bundle losses. Many companies sell offerings consisting of many individual products and services. For example, a printing company not only prints brochures but also helps design the job, matches colors, schedules the job to meet the buyer's time requirements, and so on. To maximize the perceived value, the seller should identify each of these as a separate product or service and promote the value of each one explicitly ("Look at all you get in our Deluxe Package!"), unbundling the gains. However, rather than asking the buyer to make individual expenditure decisions, the seller should identify the customer's needs and offer a package price to meet them ("One price brings everything to you!"), bundling the loss. If the buyer objects to the price, the seller can take away a service, which will then make that service appear as stand alone "loss" that will be hard to give up.[19]

Pricing on Purpose: Applying Value Pricing

You will never get paid more than you think you are worth.

An American attorney wrote about her experience and how value pricing had changed her life through improving her self-esteem. She had been admonished by her mother-in-law that men are in business to make money while women are in business to look after people and that she had to get over it. Her attitude of taking care of people had given her no satisfaction because she and her client base placed value on her help purely through the hourly billing rate. She was popular and her clients loved her; but the just was not enough. When she applied the value pricing model, she started to take her self worth seriously and priced accordingly. This hard look at what she could offer was instrumental in getting her clients to take her seriously.[20]

Now, the math. To begin, you must have a handle on your costs which is why there are chapters on costing in this book. Knowing how to produce the metrics for your company and its products or service, is the prerequisite to creating the metrics to answer the questions below — how you attach a number to some of the answers to these questions. Moreover, you will realize from these questions

19. "The Strategy and Tactics of Pricing. A Guide to Growing More Profitably", 4th ed. Nagle, T.E. and Hogan, E. H. Pearson published by Prentice Hall 2006 p. 95-101.
20. Baker, Ronald J. Pricing on Purpose. Creating and Capturing Value. John Wiley and Sons Inc. Hoboken, New Jersey. 2006 p . 318

that the salespeople will have to understand their customer intimately in order to make this process work.

- How are you helping the customer to grow their business and be more profitable?

- How are you helping the customer to reduce risk?

- How are you making the customer's business more valuable?

- How are you helping the customer achieve their targets?

- How are you removing surprises for the customer?

- At what price would the customer stop buying?

- At what price would the product or service be expensive but the customer still buy?

- At what price would your product be inexpensive?

- At what price does the pricing become so cheap that the customer questions its value?

- What price would be the most acceptable?

- At a new target price, can you make a profit above costs?

- How can you segment the market and offer different prices to different customers?

- How much business can you afford to lose due to any price increase and still maintain profit levels?

The above questions, modeled after Ronald Baker's instructive work, lists most of the questions that should be asked to determine the value-added aspects of your product or service.

Summary

In this chapter we have mainly been concerned with the viewpoint of the marketing department which instinctively downplays the role of costs.

However, we do need to revisit costs to give balance. With true costs integrated into a marketing plan, business owners can develop a fully rounded pricing policy.

6
COST-DRIVEN PRICING STRATEGIES

Determining a price by adding a factor to costs is a standard pricing strategy. The problem with this approach is that it's hard to know which costs to include and how to weight them. In this chapter I have created a summary of dozens of books and decades of work by cost accountants to try and break it down.

Early in this chapter we examine what I have called the big-box strategy of assigning variable and fixed costs as much as possible to each item on the shelf. It leads to some interesting concepts for making "super-profits."

Included are some suggestions on how to organize your profit and loss financial statements in order to tease out this information easily.

The second part of this chapter demonstrates the downside of cost-plus approaches to pricing. It is a formula for mediocrity and leaves money on the table.

And if, at the end of this chapter, you are not yet exasperated by my deconstruction, I have added some thoughts about using value as a starting point in pricing decisions.

Cost Approach Strategies

If you don't want to follow the herd, but want to make money and need a starting point from which to test your pricing strategy, you will need to know your true costs.

What is the cost of an item?

Is the cost of an item the dollar value on the invoice or catalog, or that number with the freight and taxes included? What is the cost of labor? The labor cost plus the payroll taxes? And what about heat, light, and that small item on your profit and loss statement called your paycheck?

Finding these numbers is an accounting exercise not within the realm of this book to explain in detail. However, a decent bookkeeper can respond to the following questions:

For labor:

- What is the real cost-per-hour including all payroll taxes for all the revenue-producing staff?

- What is the cost-per-hour for all non-revenue producing staff?

- What is the administrative burden cost-per-hour?

- What is this total figure and how does it compare to what you state your hourly rate to be?

For product:

- What is the dollar amount invested?

- What are the additional costs of storage, freight and handling?

- What is the annual Return on Investment (and compare that to what you could earn with that amount of cash in a bank account instead of your business)?

Now what? You have tortured your bookkeeper for three weeks to find these numbers and have them on your desk in front of you. What can you possibly do with this information?

EXAMPLE: Big-box store cost-driven pricing

Assume that a big-box store pays $150 for each electric lawn-mower and buys 1,000 for the season.

Therefore the store must write a check to the supplier for $150,000.

Then the other costs of handling, unpackaging, storing and assembling the lawnmowers will be $1580 (from historical costs).

The costs of heat and light, rent, and janitorial services per square foot total $789 for the floor area occupied by the lawn-mower display.

The store wishes to have a 25 percent return on the $150,000 invested (totaling $37,500).

We therefore have a total "cost" of $150,000 + $1,580 + $789 + $37,500 = $189,869.

But they've also calculated that not all 1,000 lawnmowers will be sold. Some will be damaged in freight, damaged in assembly or by customers, returned, or just simply won't sell. Let's say that number is 75.

So the final selling price becomes $189,869 / (1,000 − 75 = 925) = $205.26. (This is why some big-box store prices end in unconventional numbers).

TABLE 15
BIG-BOX STORE EXAMPLE

Invoice Cost per Lawnmower	$ 150.00
Quantity purchased	1000
Cheque to supplier	$ 150,000.00
Return on Investment @ 25 percent	$ 37,500.00
Handling & Storage Costs	$ 1,580.00
Utilities	$ 789.00
Total "Cost"	$ 189,869.00
Expected Damage Factor (in Units)	75
Sellable Quantity	925
Selling Price per Lawnmower	$ 205.26

At the end of the season, the store goes looking for the 75 estimated unsalable lawnmowers. Indeed, the store manager finds that 25 are beyond use and are thrown away. But 50 remain salable with a little fixing up.

At what price must these 50 lawnmowers be sold to make a profit? These can be sold at 1 cent and make a profit because all the expected profit has already been made!

Instead, the store sells them at $99.99 — well below cost — and advertises this deal. Customers perceive that the big-box store has superb prices and even though it is the end of the season, people rush in to snap up the bargain. The big-box store carries no stock through the winter.

The big store's lawnmower competition — ABC Mowers across the road — has built in a profit on the sale of every one of the same lawnmowers and by season end has 10 percent left as well. But these cannot be sold to match the big store's price because that will cut into profits. So the price does not drop, the customers see that ABC is a high-price competitor to the big store and the following spring, ABC still has last year's model on the shelf.

Of course, the big-box store not only monitors and accounts for costs but also actively seeks out and destroys costs. This frenzied attention to costs at every level has made some of the largest retailers in the world what they are today.

In the example, you can see how knowing the real costs enables you as the business owner to create strategies to build customer loyalty, open up new accounts and generate a reputation for having the best prices in town.

TIP: Looking for a way to fight the big-box stores? Undoubtedly some suppliers have found it uneconomical to supply deep discounters like Wal-Mart and Costco. But those products still need outlets where sales and after-market service are important.

TABLE 16
SYMPHONY STORY

The following is supposedly a report by a work study engineer following a visit to a symphony concert.

For considerable periods the four oboe players had nothing to do. Everyone thought the number should be reduced and the work spread more evenly over the whole concert thus eliminating the peaks of activity.

All the twelve violins were playing identical notes; this seemed to be unnecessary duplication. If a larger volume of sound was required it could be obtained by electronic means. Much effort has been absorbed in the playing of demi-semi quavers; this seems to be an unnecessary refinement. It was recommended that all the notes be rounded up to the nearest semi-quaver. If this was done, it would be possible to use trainees and lower grade operatives more extensively.

No useful purpose was served by repeating a passage on the horns which was already handled by the strings. It was estimated that if all redundant passages were eliminated, the whole concert time would be reduced from 2 hours to 20 minutes, and there would be no need for an intermission.

Since the players were provided with written instructions, the fellow at the front appeared to be redundant too.

Know Your Costs

In the big-box store example, the cost of everything from paying the rent and staff, to the electricity and air conditioning and garbage pickup are calculated and assigned on a percentage to individual inventory items to find a selling price. Although the example in Table 16 covers most of the obvious areas of concern, each trade has its own costs that need to be considered.

For example, in sheet metal manufacturing, the cost of the waste has to be taken into account. If the waste sheet metal from die punching is 12 percent, that waste cost must be rolled into the overall costs at full value. If you need price flexibility you can take into account the dollars recovered from the scrap metal merchant when you sell that 12 percent.

In fresh vegetable and fruit sales, the waste factor will vary but it has a huge impact on the final selling price. In a 2007 discussion with Ron Dust, Operations Manager for a salad provider in Kelowna, we discussed the waste percentages that are normal for the fresh produce industry. When buying standard-grade vegetables the waste is typically up to 50 percent. This means that the vegetables, with their limited shelf life, reach the end of their appeal to customers before they are sold, so they are tossed out.

In 1997, I examined a bakery in Vancouver where the gross margin was 97 percent. When I asked the owners how they did this, the two brothers showed me that they baked enough goodies for one day's sales only. Moreover they had, over many years of experimentation, come up with recipes for cookies and pastries where the finished and unsold goods could be ground up and used again in another creation the following day. Waste was thereby reduced to 3 percent.

And, to come back full circle, there are the stories of a penny-pinching president of a retail giant visiting his stores across the United States. On arrival at each local store, the president's first step would be to take the store manager to the nearest cash register station and pull from the shelves underneath all the items that were placed there over several weeks by cashiers. These were items rejected the customer at the last moment and stuffed under the counter to be dealt with later. "Here is your profit, gentlemen," the president would point out.

And what about labor costs? For those business owners with a large labor component in their business, the labor cost is not the hourly wage you pay the staff. There are payroll taxes that typically add up to an additional 25 percent. So, the $10.00 per hour warehouseman is really costing you $12.50 per hour — every hour. See the Appendix on Knowing Your Labor Costs for a full workout of the dollars involved.

Are these the only costs? If you have not studied and embraced lean manufacturing concepts, JIT[21], KanBan[22] or the Theory of Constraint concepts[23], then consider the following fictional story about "Herbies" and the potential cost to your company.

---

21. Just In Time (JIT) is an inventory strategy implemented to improve the return on investment of a business by reducing in-process inventory and its associated costs. The process is driven by a series of signals, or Kanban that tell production processes when to make the next part. Kanban are usually "tickets" but can be simple visual signals, such as the presence or absence of a part on a shelf. When implemented correctly, JIT can lead to dramatic improvements in a manufacturing organization's return on investment, quality, and efficiency.

New stock is ordered when stock drops to the reorder level. This saves warehouse space and costs. However, one drawback of the JIT system is that the reorder level is determined by historical demand. If demand rises above the historical average demand, the firm will deplete inventory faster than usual and cause customer service issues. To meet a 95 percent service rate a firm must carry about 3 standard deviations of demand in safety stock. Forecasted shifts in demand should be planned for around the Kanban until trends can be established to reset the appropriate Kanban level. Others have suggested that recycling Kanban faster can also help flex the system by as much as 10-30 percent. In recent years manufacturers have touted a trailing 13 week average as a better predictor than most forecasters could provide.

22. Kanban is a concept related to Lean or Just In Time (JIT) production, but these two concepts are not the same thing. (The Japanese word "Kanban" is a common, everyday term meaning "signboard" or "billboard" and utterly lacks the specialized meaning which this loanword has acquired in English.) According to Taiichi Ohno, the man credited with developing JIT, Kanban is a means through which JIT is achieved.

23. Goldratt, E. M. "The Goal, A process of ongoing Improvement." North River Press. Great Barrington, MA. 1984 p. 213-15

In the account, the hero was considering a manufacturing problem. But the problem was illustrated in an unusual way; a day out with a scout troop that had ended in chaos.

The problem arose when there was a line of kids on a hike in the woods. In the middle of the line was Herbie. Herbie was slower, overweight, and not too energetic. So the line of kids stretched out with those behind Herbie getting further and further away from the head of the line. The other kids had already taken the pack off Herbie's back to help him go faster, but he was still the slowest. Everybody wanted to go faster than Herbie.

The solutions examined are standard industry responses. Someone suggested a drummer to beat the pace. In a parade, for example, there aren't many gaps because everybody is marching in step. But immediately there was another problem; how to keep the kids in front of Herbie from setting a faster pace. The answer was to have Herbie beat the drum.

The next child suggested that they tie one long rope to everyone's waists like mountain climbers. No would get left behind and no one could speed up without everyone else speeding up.

This is the theory behind assembly lines and is perhaps the most cost-effective way to produce things. But not everything can be done in an assembly line fashion. So, back to the Herbie problem.

To tweak the idea it was suggested that instead, a rope needed to be attached from Herbie to the front of the line to keep everyone from running ahead. Since everyone behind Herbie was slowed by Herbie, those kids would not need to be tied.

"Herbies," therefore, are business and production constraints. They create havoc when the rest of the organization sets off at a different pace. This means that the line of kids becomes strung out over the trail with clumps of kids at the beginning and clumps at the end; a nightmare for the leader.

In production this means piles of blanks accumulating near the brake press because the shear operator can produce at four times the rates managed by the brake press. The imbalance of production rates means that every day pallets of semi-finished goods are unprofitably moved again and again. When producing ahead of schedule was stopped in a firm I worked with in Richmond, BC, the piles went away. Goods were easier to find. The forklift was profitably employed loading delivery trucks. The shear operator was given other duties after his two hours of shearing per day was completed.

Let us assume for the moment that your cost-cutting and constraint-removing programs are well underway. If you drive your costs low enough will that help your profit picture?

Unfortunately, cost-plus pricing is a tried and true formula for mediocrity. In a strong market, cost-plus pricing leads to money being left on the table. In weak markets, cost-plus leads to overpricing and lost jobs.

How does this happen?

TABLE 17
FIXED AND VARIABLE COSTS

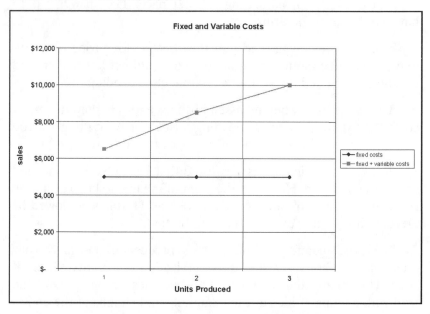

Table 17 illustrates the standard manufacturing model — the more you make the less each item costs to make. In detail, this means that the fixed costs are spread more thinly across the total number of widgets produced. Add a factor for profit and the price per unit should fall with increased production.

TABLE 18
FIXED & VARIABLE COSTS

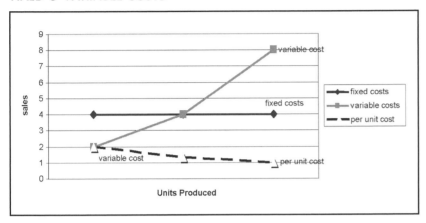

But, in a weak market, a drop in sales means the accountants will recrunch the numbers so that the fixed costs play a larger role in the total costs, putting a higher value on the costs per unit, thus driving up prices. This is intuitively opposite to what you might wish to do in a weak market.

"One particularly tragic example, for the company and its customers, was Wang Laboratory's experience in pricing the world's first word processor. Following its introduction, Wang became an instant success, growing rapidly, and dominating the market. However, as competition increased and growth slowed the company's cost driven pricing philosophy began killing its market advantage. As sales volume declined, unit costs were repeatedly recalculated and prices raised to reflect the rising overhead allocation. As a result, sales declined even further. Before long, even Wang's most loyal customers began making the switch to cheaper alternatives.

A price increase to cover higher fixed costs reduces sales further and causes unit cost to rise even further. The result is often that the price increases actually reduce profits. This leads to the "death spiral" of cost-based pricing in which fixed costs are spread continuously over declining unit volume as prices escalate even higher."[24]

What Happens in a Strong Market?

In a strong market where the accountants have control, money will surely be left on the table. In a rising market where all your

---

24. Nagle, Thomas T., Hogan, John, *Strategy and Tactics of Pricing: Guide to Grow More Profitably,* 4th edition, 2006. Reprinted by permission of Pearson Education Inc., Upper Saddle River, NJ

competitors are increasing prices, the rigidly applied cost-accounting formula means your firm will become the low-cost provider and your customers will expect you to remain so after a market correction.

In a strong market the accountants should have a monitoring role only. Prices should really be set by the marketing and sales department. Their job would be to maximize profits. Cost — unless they are selling below costs — would have no bearing. Rather, the pricing consideration would be what value the product represents to the customer, and how can they charge enough so that nothing is left on the table.

Using the cost-plus model in a strong market means that money is left on the table because marketing has not made a strong enough case that their widget warrants a higher price than the cost-plus model suggests.

In a market that moves from high to low volume sales cycles, having a value driven model leaves plenty of room for volume discounts and buying your way into new customers.

A better solution to this common enough dilemma would be to start with pricing as determined by the market and the sales staff; then subtract the profit factor and examine the costs. If the math dictates that an economy model is the most profitable then that is where the company should be positioned. If the math dictates a fully loaded, all the bells and whistles product then the company is positioned at the luxury end of the market.

"Designing products that can be sold profitably at a target price has gone in the past two decades from being unusual to being the goal at most successful companies. From Marriott to Boeing, from medical technology to automobiles, profit-leading companies now think about what market segment they want a new product to serve, determine the benefits those potential customers seek, and establish a price those customers can be convinced to pay. Then companies challenge their engineers to develop products and services that can be produced at a cost low enough to make serving that market segment profitable."[25]

So, how does this apply to your janitorial company, your renovation company or hardware store? How can you apply these concepts?

If you start with knowledge of what the customer is willing to pay for a product or service you are ahead of the competition right away:

25. Nagle, Thomas T., Hogan, John, *Strategy and Tactics of Pricing: Guide to Grow More Profitably,* 4th edition, 2006. Reprinted by permission of Pearson Education Inc., Upper Saddle River, NJ

- What is the market segment you are targeting? Is it the weekend warriors or the professional cabinet installers? Is it the accountant's offices or the franchised burger joint? Is it the older homes in districts with recent skyrocketing values or empty-nesters?

- What will the cost-conscious weekend warrior pay for his or her low-end chop saw?

With most companies there are options in the product line or list of services they have available. Typically there is the gold medal version, then a silver medal version and then a bronze medal version; each with its own list of features, advantages, and benefits. The closer you get to the bottom of the list, the fewer bells and whistles are available. For example, there is always the laser guided, $\frac{3}{4}$ horsepower, four axis adjustable chop saw. This gold medal version has a gold medal price for the serious installer. At the bottom end is the chop saw with few features, priced to appeal to the person who has a weekend job to undertake in the garage:

- Subtract your profit factor and your overheads from the price and that leaves what you need to charge for the chop saw.

- Buy the chop saw you can sell at your pre-determined profit.

In a janitorial business, what is the market segment you are targeting?

Start with the customer's expectations and budget. Your customer's budget may only allow for lobby cleaning, bathrooms and a quick wipe of the desks. Your offer of a top-to-bottom deep clean that sanitizes the phones, replaces air filters and waxes floors cannot be sold to that customer. Similarly, offering the low end package to a client looking for more service will leave money on the table, and leave you with a client who thinks he or she has made a mistake because he or she is not getting the service expected.

From the customer's budget, work backwards to what you can offer at a profit taking into consideration your cost of labor (plus the payroll taxes, and travel, and overheads) plus cleaning chemicals.

Offer the package of services you can perform at a profit within the confines of the budget.

Summary

Price can be determined by totaling all the costs and then adding a factor for profit. Capturing all the costs to find the right price can be tricky and armies of accountants have spent their lives creating formulas that make sense for their industry.

In this chapter and the appendices, we have pointed to areas to review in order to capture all the costs.

We explored the idea that cost-plus is a formula for mediocrity and leaves money on the table.

In the big-box store example, we can see how the cost information plus a return on investment factor helps determine prices. But the creative part of this costing model is the creation of super-profits by managing the layer of unsold goods.

In other industries, cost-plus should not be the only pricing method, but rather the foundation for value-driven pricing.

7
MARKETING AND SALES: WHERE YOUR PRICING DECISIONS BECOME REALITY

"How customers respond to your pricing is determined by more than the value delivered by your product and the price you charge. It is also influenced by how they evaluate your product and your price. If you leave those judgments to chance, you are likely to be paid much less or sell much less than you could…. If you want them to recognize your value, you have to make the process easier for them by supplying them with information about your offer and what you think it should mean to them." [26]

Captive Product: Finding Value in Linked Products and Services

Pricing products that must be used with the main product

Have you recently purchased a printer or a photocopier? The prices of the equipment are low. The price of the replacement ink cartridges is high. The money not made on the printer is more than made up for on the ink and toner cartridges — products that need frequent replacement.

26. Nagle, Thomas T., Hogan, John, *Strategy and Tactics of Pricing: Guide to Grow More Profitably,* 4th edition, 2006. Reprinted by permission of Pearson Education Inc., Upper Saddle River, NJ

This well-known strategy has been adopted by many companies; this is the captive product marketing strategy.

It also applies to services. In an MBA study from Simon Fraser University in 1982[27], Grant MacFarlane discovered that appliance retailers who had built a relationship with customers during the manufacturer's warranty period received the most after-warranty service calls. In other words, the warranty program that went with the purchase of the new fridge or stove captured most of the after-market for the service provider. The service customer had become accustomed to phoning the sales office for repairs long before the warranty was over and continued to do so. This item of information provided the intellectual underpinnings for the extended warranty programs that were developed by MacDonald Supply.

Another example is from when I used to sell belts and motors for repair services. The belts were inexpensive to buy and sold for a few dollars. There was never any sticker shock. The motors, on the other hand, sold for $100 or better if I followed the usual cost-based strategy. Asking more than $100 was asking the customer to cross a psychological barrier. And the sticker shock was real and palpable. Each belt and motor made a gross profit (profit X number of sales). However, I sold proportionately more belts than motors. My solution was to increase the price of the belts by a factor of 4, and to drop the price of the motor by 20 percent. In fact, I profited more using this distorted model than if I had continued to use my cost-based price structure with equal margins for belts and motors. Moreover, I no longer had the problem of sticker shock with the motors.

Meeting the Price Objection

Sticker shock is a constant in the salesperson's universe. Even if not genuinely felt, some people will fake it to set the groundwork for a price negotiation. It is sometimes a buyer's strategy.

Knowing that sticker shock reactions can be a strategy is helpful because it illuminates the path to avoiding that reaction. Customers wish to maximize value, and minimizing the price is just one way of doing that.

Your job as the business owner is to get that value on the table first. Before price enters into any discussion you must be able to show the detailed value as offered by your product or service. Once

---

27. "How Can Appliance Parts and Service be Marketed Most Effectively?" Simon Fraser University MBA Research Project, Grant MacFarlane, 1982.

the value side of the ledger is built up in the minds of your customers then the price is outweighed.

Consider the vacuum cleaner salesperson who comes into your living room and dumps a pile of dirt on your carpet. From the very beginning, that salesperson is starting from a negative position because of the bad reputation vacuum cleaner salespeople have. All the time the sales person is talking a veritable dust storm about the warranties and universal stair cleaning tools while demonstrating its incredible suction power. Price does not enter the picture until after all the buying signals have been received loud and clear. Price is not revealed until the customer has said and repeated "yes!" to a number of carefully programmed questions.

We are, of course, speaking about sales techniques. People with poor sales skills sell on price alone. The only response they have to the question "Why should I buy from your company?" is discounts. Good sales people find a way to paint a picture of value in their clients' heads.

> I hired Quincy in the summer of 1989 or thereabouts. From the very beginning I noticed that he had no difficulty selling goods to customers. This was an area that had troubled me. Each time with Quincy, however, the customer appeared to have no problem with the price. So I watched his sales technique and borrowed it. When a customer came to the counter with a $9.95 widget in hand — sticker clearly showing — and asked what HIS or HER price was, Quincy would take the widget from the customer and examine the item and the price tag. With an imp-like twinkle in his eye he would casually state the price as "$9,000 but today, with your discount, that will be $9.95." When the laughter died down, the price objection was gone and the customer paid full price.

In the early '80s I was privileged enough to watch a trainer from Maytag going through the exercise of "proving" that Maytag had enough value to justify its significantly higher price for washing machines. He talked about the attention paid during the manufacturing process to making durable components and the warranty offered. He demonstrated that the engineers had made the machine easy to repair by having its major components just behind the front panel. For the most part, this information had to be imparted to give substance to the "heavy duty" claims made by Maytag. But the crowd of sales staff was falling asleep because these facts were being delivered in engineer speak. Potential customers were only going to see an expensive metal box that washed clothes.

In response, this 340 pound trainer, while he was describing the springs and machining, stepped up a little ladder and into the washing machine, raising his arms like Rocky Balboa at the end of a fight. That woke up the crowd, as he demonstrated the machine's strength. Now they had a story to tell and a demonstration that would have customers talking about the fabulous machine they bought and not about price.

You can mold sticker shock price objections to work for you by doing a little homework. When I owned a hardware store, we started selling repair parts for barbecues. The suppliers told me that only Canadian Tire and Home Hardware sold repair parts and that they were inferior because these parts were universal replacement parts and not original equipment from the manufacturer (OEM). Nevertheless, it was part of my spring routine for several years to price shop my competition to see what they had in stock and what they charged. Since the burners for a barbecue sold in the mid 1990s for some 20 to 30 percent of the original value of the barbecue, there was sticker shock nearly every time. I watched the reaction to the sticker shock and was able to quote from my research that even though I had the OEM replacement part, my competitors across town had a suitable universal replacement that only required "some" assembly and it was $1.50 less. I could see the mental calculator going. "A little assembly is what the barbecue itself was supposed to need, and it took me a whole Saturday afternoon and a case of beer." I never lost a sale to sticker shock again.

EXAMPLE

When I had a renovation business in the early 1990s, I took a course on estimating. The point of the course was to enable me to quote a bathroom renovation, for example, in just a few minutes. That way I could gauge the sticker shock on my client's face. In one instance, I listened to the list of items the client wanted and quickly made up a quote for $5,000. The faces told me that this was more than they expected. So I asked "What did you think this might be?" They told me a lower price and I reworked the quote on the spot by replacing some "Wish List" items with more economical items to get the price down. I got the job.

Prices should really not be lowered in response to sticker shock. This response only encourages your worst customers who have no loyalty and buy elsewhere for a nickel less. It cheats your best customers who will pay full price and support your enterprise.

Rather than lowering the price, consider removing value:

- shorter warranty terms;

- no credit — cash only;

- only sell bundles of a year' s supply at once;

- unbundle the service and maintenance component;

- remove the handbag and handkerchief from the bundle;

- leave the cleanup and disposal costs to the customer;

- have the concrete deck customer do the digging out.

Finally, remember that price is an indicator of value in itself. Would diamond rings be so dramatic an indicator of commitment if they were priced at $4.95? After all, some diamonds are found just lying on the ground. Do they not have any value?

Would Nike sell any more running shoes to teenagers if they were priced at $50 instead of $150? No, a teenager's need to fit in with the crowd and not wear nerdy shoes is the price driver.

"In his book, *Influence: the New Psychology of Modern Persuasion*, Robert B. Cialdini tells of a friend who operated a native jewelry store in Arizona. She bought an allotment of turquoise jewelry but it did not sell, even during the peak tourist season. The owner subsequently went out of town but before leaving she wrote a note to her head saleswoman, "Everything in this display case, price x ½" hoping to rid herself of the offending inventory, even at a loss. Upon her return from a trip she was surprised to learn all of the jewelry had been sold. But the employee had read the "½" in the scrawled message as "2". The entire allotment had sold out at twice the original price."[28]

Push prices higher. High prices improve the experience. High prices don't just talk, they tempt.

---

28. Baker. Ronald J. Pricing on Purpose. Creating and Capturing Value. John Wiley and Sons Inc. Hoboken, New Jersey. 2006 p. 204

Sales and Promotional Pricing

Why give customers a discount for giving you their normal order? Why not save the discount for when they do something you want them to do, like place a really large order or make you their sole supplier?

Sales are a way of life for retailers and distributors alike. Sometimes they are a way of attempting to solve an in-house problem like an overstock of green peppers. Sometimes, they are to fend off outside threats like a new competitor. Sometimes they are to introduce a new model or line of clothing. Sometimes, sales are just a habit. Sometimes they are to keep the company name in the paper and in front of customers' eyes.

There are only a few good reasons to have a sale:

To facilitate the sale of one or two weak products by discounting an entire product line

If, in your product line, there are items that just don't sell, consider using BOGOF (Buy One Get One Free) as a version of bundling to move one unpopular item bundled together with one popular item. Or, if you have a line of windbreakers where only certain sizes and colors are selling, consider a sale on the entire line to entice potential customers.

To spur declining sales, create more store traffic or grow the customer list

Most retailers count the number of people coming through their doors or the number of invoices written to get a picture of the interest generated by their advertising or general location.

Increasing the number of people through the doors by finding new market segments is laudable. Each new and added customer is a sales and profit opportunity.

However, improving traffic through the doors without improving the profit per customer is a sure indicator of a muddled idea. If increasing the pairs of feet is important, consider putting the promotional items at the back of the store so that the customers see lots of products on the way. This is the strategy behind grocery stores always having the milk (no margin) at the back of the store. On the way, the customer picks up a package of cookies (great margin) and that drain cleaner (great margin) they have been forgetting to pick up.

On a recent consulting contract in Kelowna, I encouraged the owners to measure the dollar value per customer in their bakery. At the beginning, the average sale per customer was $4. By focusing on this number, sales per customer steadily rose over 8 months to $5. The staff upsold customers on the specially marked impulse items to be sold that day. Not much you may say, but with over 100 customers per day coming through the doors that meant $100 a day more revenue for merely paying attention to this one measure. This led inevitably to merchandising efforts to place impulse goods within reach at the cash counter and a bit more friendly promotional chat from the sales staff.

Market penetration — to introduce a new product and gain immediate market share

With this strategy it is usual to set a low initial price in order to penetrate the targeted market quickly and deeply to win a large market share. But this only works well with an established product or service when:

- the market is highly price sensitive

- production and distribution costs fall as sales volume increases

- low price keeps out the competition

Of course, if the market is not price sensitive, you have left dollars on the table. Once you have lowered prices, it is difficult to raise them again.

And if production costs do not fall with increased volumes — your plant has to work overtime, maintenance of machinery rises to record levels and your suppliers cannot give better raw material prices — then your strategy will falter due to lack of supply.

If your competitors can easily follow your low price just by printing a new flyer or by distributing a memo to the sales staff, then your price-only strategy will create a situation where the industry-wide price will be low and perhaps not profitable for anyone.

To get rid of slow-moving inventory

Converting slow-moving inventory into cash to buy fast-moving inventory should be a constant activity in any inventory-based business. Too many companies allow their retail items to get covered in dust, stale dates to lapse, and labeling to become worn out, making customers believe that they are shopping in the wrong store. If no one else wants it, it must be overpriced, or trash.

If this sounds like you, price it to get rid of it and recover as much of your cost as possible. Even if you only get back what you spent, then at least you can turn that into something better.

For example, if a certain make of paper towel is on your shelves after three years, it is likely that it will never sell. If it could be sold at cost, giving up all the profit, then the cash could be used to buy fast-moving cases of paper towels.

To encourage the concentration of purchases

Perhaps it is to your advantage to sell a year's worth of plastic buckets on one invoice to your customer. You won't be able to sell him or her anything for a year afterwards, but neither will the competition. And perhaps you can claw back some of the discount you offered by having lower freight costs to get the product in the door.

But sometimes you need a sale to achieve the opposite. In Richmond, I knew the owner of a lawnmower repair shop. From April to September he would work day and night, seven days a week to clear a six week backlog of mowers that came in for repair. One year, in a fit of organization, he wrote to all of his customers and offered that should they bring the mowers into the shop before Christmas, he would give them a break on the price, have the machine ready for the first mow of the season and store them in the meantime. It was a wild success that spread his workload over many months and allowed for rushed customers to get their mowers repaired without long delays.

To reward long-term customers for good behaviour

Reduced prices to reward long-term customers or customer responses such as paying early or promoting the product are other reasons you might want to have a sale.

Beware: Sometimes, companies have sales just because their suppliers have sales. The motivation of the supplier could be any one of the above reasons. Beware that you do not become the victim of a sale that does not benefit your company directly.

Also, promotions may temporarily reduce sales to existing customers. According to a three year study done by MIT in 2004,[29] promotional pricing is a double-edged sword. In their study they sent out standard priced catalogues to one-third of the customer list, a shallow discounted catalogue to the next third and finally a deep-discount catalogue to the final third. In the short term, the strategy harvested new customers but in the long term the regular customers bought less. Why?

The authors discerned a pattern whereby the deep promotion got new customers as was wanted by the business. However, deep discounts to existing customers worked in reverse because customers appeared to have stocked up when the prices were low, satisfying their needs. They did not return to their normal buying habits for some time.

The moral of the story is to know your customers. If you want customers to buy bathroom fixtures don't send deep-discount promotions to those who regularly buy bathroom fixtures. Better to send those customers a promotion about roofing or tile floors.

Beware the Boxing Day Sale Syndrome

For many years the major department stores in Vancouver had massive Boxing Day sales. They were the talk of the town with giveaway prices and queues of anxious customers for blocks. But after a while, the public caught on to this and sales prior to Christmas fell. Would you buy a $1,000 stereo system before Christmas if two days later you could buy it for $99?

Gillette created a similar problem in the 1990s when its management and sales team focused on growing its sales volumes. Each month meant a huge amount of time and effort spent scrutinizing sales trend. If the targets were in danger the call would go out to the sales staff for "one-time only" discount offers. Of course, the "one-off discount" became a pattern and customers stopped buying at the beginning of the month and waited for the month end discounts.[30]

29."Does Promotional Pricing Grow future Business? Deep discounting Strategies provide decidedly mixed long term benefits." Eric Anderson and Duncan Simester. MIT Sloan Management Review. Summer 2004. Vol. 45.
30. Nagle, Thomas T., Hogan, John, *Strategy and Tactics of Pricing: Guide to Grow More Profitably*, 4th edition, 2006. Reprinted by permission of Pearson Education Inc., Upper Saddle River, NJ

Beware of undermining morale

If you have ever negotiated the purchase of a car in a showroom then you will understand that price flexibility increases the higher up the ladder you go. In the event that a discount offered by the salesperson to get the sale is required, then beware of undermining your salesperson's morale by allowing the sales manager to offer even larger discounts. The following is an account by John Winkler about how one company solved the problem of handling customers who understood that discounts got deeper the higher up you go in the command chain.[31]

The franchise Mr. Winkler examined negotiated sites and franchise renewals with each franchise holder every five years. One area sales manager was responsible for the renewals and for demanding capital investment for existing and new sites. If the franchise holder got difficult with these demands, he or she might insist on seeing the Sales Director. The area sales manager with whom the negotiations had proceeded typically told the demanding franchise holder that this was possible but that the Sales Director was a very difficult person. However, if he or she still wanted that to happen then it would be arranged. This was all part of the plan.

When the Sales Director attended the meetings he was always polite and charming to the franchise holder. However, partway through the meeting the Sales Director suddenly told the franchise holder that there was something about a particular concession the area sales manager had already made that he did not like. At this point the initial demands by the franchise holder suddenly took back seat to a threat to the franchise renewal. Far from acceding to the franchisee's extra demands, the Sales Director was now indicating that the company could not possibly honor the areas sales manager's concession. He would need time to rethink the deal completely.

By now the franchisee was panicking because he or she saw the threat to the existing contract. Later, the area manager re-entered the negotiations, restored the concession, smoothed the waters and closed the deal. As expected, the franchise holder never wanted to meet the Sales Director again and always preferred to deal with the area sales manager.

---

31. John Winkler. Pricing for Results. Facts on File Publications. New York. 1983 p. 103

Price Discrimination

Price discrimination exists. You and I pay different prices for goods than some other buyers and we pay higher prices at certain times of the day or week than at other times. For example, it appears from a casual study of the price of gasoline that it rises for summer long weekends.

Sound unfair? Some people would describe it that way. Moral outrage is well beyond the scope of this book and we are, after all, dealing with reality, not utopia. From a business owner perspective, you can mine profit where none existed before by finding these profit opportunities.

Consider the NEXUS lane at the US/Canada border crossing. For a fee, you can bypass the long lineup in moments, while those who did not pay the fee are left to wait considerably longer.

Consider coupons — if you take the time to hunt them down, clip them out and present them, you get a price break.

Consider beer. Some pints are sold at happy hour prices, some of it at normal prices.

In "The Golden Vein,"[32] a June 2004 article in the Economist Technology Quarterly, the writer found an unlikely application for the latest in data mining. The traditional British pub, in the hands of some sophisticated owners, can now change the prices of different drinks from day to day, by using software that assesses the impact that "happy hour" offers have on sales. How do they apply this? If a discount on a particular brand of beer boosts sales one day, it is likely to remain discounted the next — and if not, something else will be offered. The term "data mining," is used to describe the application of technology to this simplest of businesses, and is being replaced by "business intelligence". Of course, this kind of data collection requires many other elements to be in place, such as the capacity to track inventory accurately and re-price products dynamically.

And what can you make of crazy airline ticket pricing? What has cost to do with staying over for a Saturday night or booking weeks in advance? Doesn't it cost just as much to fly a child as it does an adult? The following joke circulated for a few months and I remember it for its familiar caricature of the business of buying a ticket.

---

32. "The Golden Vein" The Economist Technology Quarterly. June 2004

IF AIRLINES SOLD BREAD

Customer: Hi. How much is a loaf of your bread?

Store Clerk: Well, sir, that depends on a lot of things.

Customer: Well, is there an average price?

Store Clerk: Our lowest price is $2 a loaf, and we have 60 different prices up to $200 a loaf.

Customer: Is there a difference in the bread quality?

Store Clerk: No difference; it's all the same bread.

Customer: Well, then I'd like some of that $2 bread.

Store Clerk: When do you intend to use the bread?

Customer: I want to eat it tomorrow.

Store Clerk: Sir, the bread for tomorrow is the $200 bread.

Customer: When would I have to buy to get the $2 bread?

Store Clerk: You would have to make sandwiches and eat them very late at night in about 3 weeks. But you will have to agree to start eating the sandwiches before Friday of that week and continue eating until at least Sunday.

Customer: You've got to be kidding!

Store Clerk: I'll check and see if there's any bread available.

Customer: You have shelves full of bread! I can see it!

Store Clerk: But it doesn't mean that we have bread available. We sell only a certain number of loaves on any given weekend. Oh, and by the way, the price per loaf just went to $16. We don't have any more $2 bread.

Customer: The price went up as we were talking?

Store Clerk: Yes, sir. We change the prices and rules hundreds of times a day, and since you haven't actually walked out of the store with your bread yet, we just decided to change them. I suggest you purchase your bread as soon as possible. How many loaves do you want?

Customer: Well, maybe five loaves. Make that six, so I'll have enough.

Store Clerk: Oh no, sir, you can't do that. If you buy bread and don't use it, there are penalties and possible confiscation of the bread you already have.

Customer: WHAT?

Store Clerk: We can sell enough bread for sandwiches for your entire family but if one family member switches to spaghetti before the bread is completely finished, then you will lose your remaining loaves of bread.

Customer: Why does it matter whether I use all the bread? I already paid you for it!

Store Clerk: We make plans based upon the idea that all of our bread is used, every slice. If you don't use it all, it causes us all sorts of problems.

Customer: This is crazy! I suppose something terrible happens if I don't keep making and eating sandwiches until after Saturday night!

Store Clerk: Oh yes! Every loaf you bought automatically becomes the $200 bread.

Customer: But what are all these, "Bread on sale from $1 a loaf" signs?

Store Clerk: Well, that's for our budget bread. It only comes in half-loaves. $1 will only make one and half sandwiches. The second half-loaf to complete the sandwich is $20. None of the wrappers have labels, some are empty and there are no refunds, even on the empty wrappers.

Customer: The heck with this! I'll buy what I need somewhere else!

Store Clerk: I don't think so, sir. You might be able to buy bread for your weekend sandwiches from someone else, but you won't be able to get bread for sandwiches for weekdays from anyone but us. And I should point out, sir, that if you make open-faced sandwiches, it will be $300 a loaf.

Customer: I thought your most expensive bread was $200!

Store Clerk: That's if you make normal sandwiches. Bread rolls are different.

Customer: And if I buy $200 bread for the weekend, but use some rolls from the freezer to dip in my soup, you'll confiscate the remainder of my bread?

Store Clerk: No, we'll charge you an extra-use fee plus the difference on your next loaf of bread. But I believe you're getting it now, sir.

Customer: You're insane!

Store Clerk: Thanks for buying bread from AirUs.

No two airline tickets are the same — it all depends on when you purchase your ticket, whether there are layovers, whether you are travelling for business or pleasure, and other rules that are put in place to establish the value you place on your airline flight.

So, is price discrimination fair and right? Although this question is commonly asked, it belongs more in the realm of philosophy than the real world of business. It is more fruitful and helpful to consider that price discrimination —

- is all around us and is a constant in the business universe;

- has always been with us and probably always will be;

- actually benefits some sectors of the population;

- can be a rich source of profits for the savvy businessperson.

On Customer Behavior
The simple truth about why people buy & why they don't buy

Business speaker and coach Donald Cooper has a unique way of understanding fundamental business truths. Here is his take on why people buy, and why they don't buy.

"You could fill a large room with all the books ever written on the subject of why people buy and why they don't buy and, mostly, they over-confuse the issue. The simple truth is that people buy "stuff" (products and services), in every part of their business and their personal lives for one reason only: To make some of their stress go away.

That's it! Whatever you sell, whether it's groceries, computers, insurance, club memberships, vacations, production equipment, or private jets; whatever it is, people buy your "stuff" to reduce some physical or emotional stress in their lives. Therefore, your real job is to be a stress remover.

Stress is a "pull-push" phenomenon. There are stresses in peoples' lives that pull or attract them to what you sell, and there are also stresses that prevent them from buying what you sell, or buying it specifically from you.

So, here's a valuable little exercise that's well worth doing. Sit down for one hour with a small group of your brightest and most caring people and finish these three sentences:

1. The physical and emotional stresses in our target customers' lives that attract them to buy what we sell are …

2. The physical and emotional stresses that could prevent them from buying what we sell are …

3. The stresses that we create in our business that could prevent our target customers from buying specifically from us are …

Once you understand what stresses are "attracting" and "preventing" your target customers, get creative. How can you reinvent your business to dramatically emphasize the stresses that attract people to what you sell and how can you boldly eliminate the "preventors" that could be keeping them from buying what you sell, or buying it specifically from you?

Here's a real-life example to show you how powerful this process can be.

One of our clients, a very successful travel agency, addressed the three questions above and came up with hundreds of insights, one of which was that the fear of flying could be a stress preventing some people from becoming customers. One of his staff came up with the idea of offering a seminar on this subject with the help of a local psychologist. They promoted the event with the help of local radio, TV and newspapers. It attracted many new clients; they now offer the course twice each year … and the media coverage has helped make them famous!"[33]

---

33. Donald Cooper. Used with permission.

There are other types of customer behavior, of course. If you have been in business more than five minutes, you will know that there are saints and sinners among your customers. And you may be vaguely aware that the sinners take up more of your time than all the saints combined.

There is nothing worse for your firm's morale than to continue to serve customers who do not understand or appreciate the value you provide. Given a choice between continuing a relationship with a toxic customer and the effect it will have on the morale of your team members, observe who former CEO of Southwest Airlines, Herb Kelleher, sided with, as this story from "Nuts! Southwest Airlines' Crazy Recipe for Business and Personal Success" illustrates:

A woman frequently flew on southwest, but was disappointed with every aspect of the company's operation. In fact, she became known as the Pen Pal because after every flight she wrote in with a complaint. It was quickly becoming a problem for customer service staff until someone fully sent her letter up to Herb's desk, with a note: "This one's yours."

In 60 seconds, Kelleher wrote back and said, "Dear Mrs. Crabapple. We will miss you. Love, Herb."

Beware: Your customers are not going to improve until you do, so consider improving your company's morale by deciding which customers are actually toxic.

On Keeping Customers

In a study reported by Right Technologies called the Loyalty Connection, Bob Thompson suggests that the perception of why customers leave is different for customers as opposed to business owners.

In his analysis customers leave almost 75 percent of the time due to customer service problems, while owners see that as being important in only 22 percent of the cases.

Quality is an issue to customers 32 percent of the time while owners rank quality as the suspect only 18 percent of the time.

It appears that staff indifference is a greater cause of losing customers than doing a bad job altogether.

Similarly and most importantly, pricing was ranked by owners as the number one issue at 45 percent, while customers actually left because of price only 25 percent of the time.

An intriguing indicator is that 35 percent of customers noted their "needs changed," but business owners saw that as being relevant only 8 percent of the time. Perhaps the businesses are out of touch with their own customer base?

So training your staff and sales people — are they all selling some aspect of the business? — should be your number one priority.

Sales Training

Never lose an opportunity to train sales staff. Salespeople will inevitably mention price too soon if not fully equipped with a good sales presentation that speaks to the customer's needs.

Louis J. De Rose, author of "The Value Network; Integrating the Five Critical Processes That Create Customer Satisfaction" had an interesting insight into the use of language in controlling our response to pricing and selling. In his 2004 article entitled "Value Selling," he started with a quote from the Austrian philosopher, Ludwig Wittgenstein, who said: "He who controls vocabulary, controls thought". De Rose then went on to add that implicit in this pearl of wisdom is that he who controls thought, controls action. What De Rose mean is that if you can gain acceptance of the meaning of words and phrases you employ in your sales and marketing, you go a long way to mastering the buying situation.

From his consulting and training experience, De Rose felt that few salespeople truly appreciate the role of vocabulary in controlling the buying situation. Why, and what does this mean?

First, salespeople too often allow the customer to downplay the company's product or service to the level of a commodity. Essentially, allowing that to happen means that when the buying decision is based on competition between commodity offerings, low price must be the purchase-determining factor. By failing to challenge the concept of leveling everything to the same low status as expressed in the words themselves, the salesperson loses the initiative in the selling process.

Second, the vocabulary salespeople employ tends to be product- service-, or technology-focused, hoping that the customer will follow:

- "Our sheet metal processes work to tolerances similar to those in a machine shop."

- "We specialize in quick-turn work. We can get you a quote in 8 hours or less."

- "We have a new paint spray unit that churns out one truck cab every 14 minutes."

By themselves, these may be highly commendable and desirable capabilities. But what do they do for the customer? How do they provide value? Does any one of them get a signature on a purchase order? Where is the call to action?

Your company's words and phrases must vividly illustrate how any one of the above will benefit the customer. If tight tolerances are not on your customer's shopping list, then this selling feature will not create any benefit. If delivery of the order is required in 45 days, then quick turnaround is not creating a benefit to the customer either. And why would anyone care about how fast you can spray a truck cab?

Your sales staff are whistling in the wind if there is a mismatch between the demand of your potential customer and what you say you are offering. Unless you can demonstrate how these capabilities reduce cost to the customer, avoid it, or offset it by increasing his or her revenue or cash flow, you're wasting breath.

Another failure is the notion that one size fits all. Too many sales presentations are canned, are read robotically and too obviously have been rehearsed to the rapt attention of the family Labrador bribed to be the pretend customer. The spiel uses one set of concepts, words, and phrases to address all those whom the sales people contact in the customer organization. The reality, in industrial markets, is that customers are rarely single purchasers. Rather, the purchasing will happen when the perceived needs of the managers, engineers, budget department and warehouse people are met. Moreover, as De Rose so elegantly pointed out, the prime driving force in defining perceptions is how they are evaluated by their superiors. How are they measured? What are the criteria by which they're promoted, compensated, downgraded, or even dismissed? A prime consideration for a designer is not one for a plant manager. Where price may be a low priority to a project manager, it is high priority to a purchasing manager.

Mr. De Rose's point is, I believe, that each selling situation must take into account the audience so that the salesperson selects the right feature and benefit. By emphasizing the benefit and thereby taking control over the vocabulary, the competition's product or service must follow suit into situations where they are at a noticeable disadvantage. Although one-sized vocabulary will not fit all buying situations, it does take hard work to find the correct words to use in a selling situation in order to have the features and benefits create the most impact.

A sales opportunity can most easily be converted into a sale when the needs of the customer are best understood. To influence a sale most effectively, the salesperson must know and understand how what his or her company is selling could be used in the customer's products or how critical it is to the performance of the customer's products.

Is it just a coffee shop selling expensive coffee? The founder of Starbucks used to tell inquisitive business writers that they built the Starbuck's brand first with the people, not with consumers — the opposite approach from that of the car and breakfast cereal companies. Starbucks' philosophy took them in the direction that the best way to meet and exceed the expectations of customers was to hire and train great people. So the CEO set out to find and invest in employees who were zealous about good coffee.[34]

Managing a customer's expectations is a large part of contract work when the price is not stickered on the item. Sometimes there is "sticker shock" from customers who plainly have no idea that cars no longer sell for $500. Your company may be the first company to tell them the raw truth.

A British Columbia-based cleaning company was recently forced to hike its prices substantially in the face of labor shortages. Of course, customers were still blissfully unaware that prices and labor rates had jumped. When the customers started laughing at quoted prices on the phone, they had to find a way to deal with this quickly so that sales would not get discouraged. Training the sales staff with the company Unique Selling Proposition solved some of the

34. Baker. Ronald J. *Pricing on Purpose. Creating and Capturing Value.* John Wiley and Sons Inc. Hoboken, New Jersey. 2006 p. 241

problem. Then they moved to showing how this carefully crafted USP added value for the customer. Finally, they moved to dealing with objections and sticker shock.

Nine Guidelines for Presenting Your Price

Do not give your price first

The first thing you should know is to leave price until last. Those customers who press for pricing right out of the gate are not interested in anything else. They have to be told politely and bluntly that if price is the only consideration, then the company offers more than they may wish to pay for.

The better approach to persuading the customer is to ask a lot of questions that demonstrate that your company knows what it is talking about and has the best interests of the customer at heart. At some point the question of what happened to the last supplier has to be asked. This is the killer question because it tells you the customer's sensitive areas. The response to customer complaints about your competitor have to be similar to "yes, we had that problem too but we fixed that a while ago," or, "I'm sorry to hear that, I hope they got it right in the end." Each complaint about your competitor will tell you what makes your client tick and reinforces the decision they made to call you.

Even if you have the lowest prices in town, the customer might still have doubts about quality, so a presentation that satisfies all these doubts must be made before price is discussed.

Remember you are looking for collaboration, not conflict.

Make the customer open, if you can

You as the supplier will have the edge if you can get the potential customer to reveal what he or she thinks will be the right price. Questions such as "What are you paying now?," or "What did you think it might cost?," or "What is your budget?" are all great ways to get information.

Make the buyer work hard

At any objection, ask the buyer why it's important. Make the buyer justify the objection so that you are uncovering information to help you with the final price. Price objections are not usually just a "no," there is always more behind the response that, uncovered, will reveal the motivations of your customer. In the sales world, a negative response is treated as a request for further information.

Sandwich your price between the benefits

Whether in person or in writing, the price should come between the first list of benefits and the last list of benefits.

An example: "This car is stylish, has all the features you listed, the colour your wife likes, and the only one you have driven today that puts a smile on your face. The price is $32,560 and we can arrange zero percent financing for you to keep the payments low."

Or, "This software package performs all of the functions you have asked for, plus there are added features that will be available to use as you get familiar with it. The price is $239 and it comes with an easy installation CD and 6 months of free support."

Try to make your price non-negotiable

Don't give any indications early on in the sales discussions that there might be price flexibility. If tested, say that it is very unlikely that prices will be different than quoted.

The cost penalties of not buying

Keep track of the benefits of the product or service you are offering as the benefits become apparent. Place a dollar value on them if possible. "So it takes your shipper 6 hours to do that job and our service would save 4 of those hours? At $15 per hour, that is $60 in one week and over 50 weeks that would be $3,000, right?"

Adding up the benefits at the end puts a dollar value penalty on not buying from you.

Don't squeeze too hard against the weaknesses

Don't be a shark. You might wish to have a repeat customer or a referral. If you have the customer over a barrel, taking full advantage will leave a nasty taste in his or her mouth.

Let the customer win something

So you fought over the price and won. Now is the time to make a friend, not an enemy. Let the customer win something small you have saved for the end, but don't just give it away. Let the customer fight for it and then you should lose gracefully.

Finally, ask for the sale

Too many salespeople forget this important part of the sales process. Presenting all the benefits and features in the world will not get the sale if you do not ask for it. If possible, it is best to assume that the sale is already made. We have all heard in the common phrase "Will that be cash or credit?"

But what if your prices are high and you are targeting the premium end of the market?

In a rising labor market, some prices rise fast. And the person used to paying small amounts for some products or services will not be happy to be confronted by a price tag that is much higher than the amount he or she has been paying.

It is wise to prepare the customer early. In the 1980s Nescafe sales representatives used to approach potential customers with the opening line "I am here to tell you why you should buy the most expensive instant coffee on the market." This is a useful statement that can be adapted to almost any industry. By referring to the benefits early you can launch into the list, eliciting responses from the customer as you go.

The Value of Persistence

Many companies honor the year's top salesperson for the company. In one story, a fellow was called to the podium from the group of hundreds of sleek, well groomed and confident car salesmen. To the sound of a collective intake of breath, a weedy, bespectacled and thoroughly unimpressive man who spoke with a weak and unconfident voice accepted the award. When asked how he became the company's top salesman, he responded that he just used the sales book as he had been trained to do. He opened the book at page one and after going through the features of the car, would, as per his sales training, ask the customer if he or she wanted to buy. If the answer was no, the he would go to page two. At the end of page two he would again ask the customer if he or she wanted to buy. If no, then he went to page three. At this point, the president of the company got impatient and asked what happened if he got to the last page and the customer said no for the final time. "Then, Mr. President, I return to page one and start again."

I have always used this story to illustrate the value of persistence. But the story also has value because scripting expresses the benefits and features of a product so that nothing is missed (you don't know what is important to a customer). Moreover, the benefits are expressed in the most positive way. To describe a car as having good tires is mediocre. To say that the car is equipped with top of the line Michelin all-weather radials, showing the Michelin picture of a baby sitting inside a tire, uses the Michelin brand image to create a fuller picture of the benefits the customer is buying.

Pocket Price Banding

Price banding is defined by the upper and lower limit at which your goods and services are sold.

"The width and shape of a pocket price band tells a fruitful story. Managers are invariably surprised not only by the width of their pocket price bands but also by the identity of the customers at the extremes of the band."[35]

What does this mean? Pocket price is the dollar ending up in the company pocket as true revenue after the price has cascaded from list to customer discount, to early payment discount, to volume rebates and to free delivery. The very flexibility in the price band means that an identical product will be sold on the same day in the same city at very different prices. And the price may vary as much as 25 percent from upper to lower limits as in an extreme case like the Castle Battery study in Chapter 11.

Moreover, the Castle Study investigated the supposition that volume pricing offered to big customers caused the variation, but found that wasn't the case. Some legacy clients who bought small amounts were regularly being given pricing similar to that offered to the largest accounts.

How does this happen? It is the familiar story of starting with a price list and then giving some flexibility to the sales force in order

---

35. Michael V. Marn and Robert L. Rosiello. *Managing price, gaining Profit.* Harvard Business Review. Sept-Oct. 1992

to get the sale. When the list price is discounted and then off-invoice costs are added, price flexibility becomes the norm rather than the exception. This could be the result of customers knowing your entire sales system too well and working the system to their advantage, or it could be due to weak selling.

Bundling and Unbundling

Bundling is the sale of goods and services lumped together to make an attractive package, where the customer is made to feel that he or she received value for money.

The simplest examples are gift baskets where the sum of the individual components is less than the selling price of the total basket.

The bundling tactic can be employed to get slow moving inventory off the shelves by tying the sale to a fast moving item and wrapping everything up in fancy paper as a gift. (People often spend more on a gift than on themselves.)

This tactic can be employed with services as well. If you are faced with customers to whom only the price per hour you charge is the deciding factor in the buying decision, then creating "price packages" makes it difficult for the customer to compare apples to apples. For example, if your regular charge-out rate is $30 per hour and the potential customer is only mildly interested in the services you have to offer for that price, repackaging at a lump price where the items are carefully delineated with enticing descriptions and a lump sum price should overcome price objections. After all, it is the check that has to be written by the customer that is important here, and with an open-ended per hour charge, the final price isn't decided until you have finished.

Unbundling is the reverse of the process wherein the series of goods offered are separated and priced separately. Typically this reveals that some service — after sales service, for example — or a gasket that is always thrown away and never used, can be removed from the package safely and sold separately. This allows for a price decrease to meet stiffer competition or to add to margins in the event that prices are not reduced.

"Consider Techco, a leading computing and software company with a broad product line. Although Techco was a recognized market

leader in technical support and breadth of selection, the company was experiencing price erosion and lost market share due to smaller competitors that competed primarily on price. While customers turned to Techco for their complex purchases that required extensive technical support, they negotiated steep discounts on other products by threatening to take their business to the low-end competitor. Management initially viewed this as a pricing problem and prepared to change their operating model to compete as a low-cost provider. Once the management had evaluated their pricing strategy more completely, however, it became clear that the underlying cause of lost sales and lower margins was a price structure that forced all customers to engage Techco in identical ways even though they had a wide variety of service needs. Customers that received little value from Techco's service were asked to pay the same price as customers who received tremendous value. As a result, Techco under-priced to its high-value customers and overpriced to its low-value customers.

The profit maximizing solution to this pricing challenge was not a wholesale reduction in prices. Instead, the solution was to redesign the priced structure in a way that allowed customers to choose how they engaged with Techco. Customers that got little value from Techco' s services were not asked to pay for them, nor were they allowed free access to service and support — an important change from past practice. Eliminating support to some customers enabled Techco to increase support to high value customers to justify higher prices. By adopting a comprehensive approach to pricing strategy, Techco was able to increase volume in the low-end segments while improving margins in the high-end segments."[36]

Learning to Lose a Percentage of Sales

In contracting, giving estimates and converting estimates to jobs is a way of life. Some businesses seem to get all the jobs. Some get the cream. Some struggle to convert any at all.

No matter how you slice and dice it, price is an important part of the package that the client considers before buying. A no-frills package at the lowest price in town may be the marketing position the company adopts to be a success. But this means the company must give —

- fanatical attention to keeping costs down,

---

36. Nagle, Thomas T., Hogan, John, *Strategy and Tactics of Pricing: Guide to Grow More Profitably,* 4th edition, 2006. Reprinted by permission of Pearson Education Inc., Upper Saddle River, NJ

- the right estimate every time, and

- no promises in order to keep customer expectations to a minimum.

The downside is that customer expectations are not always manageable and that costs have a habit of creeping up behind us.

So how to escape being the El-Cheapo of the deck-building market? Add more frills and make a fuss of customers with higher expectations. Then you get to charge more and that will presumably give you an allowance for unexpected costs.

The Winner's Curse

Consider that you are one of two bidders for a job and you give the lowest bid and win the job. Are you happy? Most likely. But what if you are the winner and lowest bidder among a dozen estimates? Are you still happy?

Most likely you would have the awful feeling that you have overlooked some costly detail.

Nagle and Hogan explain in their book on pricing[37] that in their opinion if there are many bidders, you will likely lose money if you get the job. Why? In the big picture, you are most likely to win the jobs you underestimate and lose the jobs you overestimate. Issuing lots of bids where there are lots of competitors increases your statistical chances of winning every losing job. With many bids on the table the buyer will look to the lowest bid, thereby increasing your chances of having overlooked some factor that will erode your profit. With a smaller number bids on the table, your price has a better statistical chance of being profitable.

The only solution to this is, in effect, to formalize the principle of "selective participation." Add a fudge factor to each bid to reflect and estimate how much you are likely to have underestimated your costs if you actually win a bid. Needless to say, adding this factor will reduce the number of bids you win, but it will ensure that you don't ultimately regret having won them.

---

37. Nagle and Hogan quoted in Baker. Ronald J. "Pricing on Purpose. Creating and Capturing Value." John Wiley and Sons Inc. Hoboken, New Jersey. 2006 p. 264

And What of That Feeling That You May Have Left Money on the Table?

Some customers will not buy. These may be the customers who are cranky or demanding and who you don't want. Some may be exactly the client base you want and they will walk away telling you that the price is too high.

What to do?

If you get 100 percent of the estimated jobs then your price is too low or you have a monopoly (but will not for long).

Every business has its peculiarities but roughly speaking, if you bid on three jobs and get one, then your price is likely just right.

But if you bid on 100 and get none, you are out of business because it's likely your prices are too high. Go back to the drawing board and reexamine your price list. Cut some frills or costs or reduce your product expectations.

The quest in a contracting business should be to build a good customer list, learn to identify the bad customers and not work yourself to death making quotes for people you should not be entertaining. This entails homework beforehand. A little research can yield whether or not the customer is genuine or just shopping around. More enquiries — "What happened to your last contractor?" — will yield whether they are unreasonable, picky, or a customer that sees value. Pay attention to complaints about past providers. These are the value indicators that you will need to pay attention to in order to succeed.

EXAMPLE

Contractor: What happened to the last guy doing the concrete work?

Customer: Those guys were useless. They were always late. The job was late. Then those crooks used substandard concrete. I lost money on the job.

Contractor: So in my bid, we can put in a penalty clause if we are late. Would that make you less worried?

Customer: I guess so. But what about the concrete?

Contractor: If we provide you with documents from the plant showing the quality parameters you ordered and therefore the quality of concrete we provided, would that make your engineers happy?

Customer: Yeah, it would. Let's discuss this penalty clause …

Notice in the above exchange that the bid is still under consideration. Learning what the customer wants and what his or her red button indicators are is just as important as the price.

It is worthwhile to keep a mortality log of your bidding history. Not only is the ratio of losses to wins important, but also why the job was won or lost. Of particular interest are the value factors. Was the job won because of the value you had offered in the bid — value apart from price? Or was it lost because the value you believed you had included was not important to the customer?

Remember that losing a bad customer is a good thing. Gaining 100 percent of your bids means that you are taking on the "sinners" from someone else's customer list. And your company is, after all, the sum of its customer list. Wouldn't you entertain more seriously a plumbing bid from the company that plumbed the CN Tower than some company you've never heard of with a tiny ad in the Yellow Pages?

Selling Best, Better, Good

It is a standard mantra of selling to offer the best and most expensive items first. This gives the salesperson the opportunity to explain all the bells and whistles in full.

If the customer says the price is a bit beyond their expectations, you can move down a level by removing items or features. If the customer is still hesitating, you can sell the cheapest or most economical by removing more benefits and features.

EXAMPLE 1

A chemical salesman had a successful career selling cleaning chemicals in Western Canada. His home office was decorated with award after award testifying to his considerable abilities. When I asked him how it was done in a commodity business like that he told me the secret was to extol the virtues of the product and its benefits. Then he asked for an order of one skid of four-45 gallon drums. Sometimes the answer was yes, but mostly it was no.

So, Plan B was to acknowledge that this was a little too much and ask how much the customer would like. Usually the answer was one drum or perhaps a half-skid of cases.

His point was that offering one gallon first and then trying to get the quantities up was a losing strategy that would not have earned him all the shiny awards.

EXAMPLE 2

A retailer of hearing aids was facing strong competition in his home market. His price list came from a competitor and there were enough lines on the price list to confuse most people.

After reconsidering the list, the owner developed a program to spend the better part of his sales pitch highlighting the features and benefits of the most expensive hearing aid he could sell.

If the customer complained about the price, the owner moved on to the next best hearing aid which had fewer features and benefits, but had a lower price.

If this was not acceptable, then he moved to the third hearing aid that had yet fewer features and a yet lower price. Remember that this was still the same basic hearing aid with the same reputation for quality and reliability.

There was a more economical aid below the third hearing aid, but it was the bottom of the line and most people bought before he had to sell on price alone.

EXAMPLE 3

In October of 1999, Coca-Cola faced an outcry when it announced that it was distributing new vending machines that would increase prices as the temperature rose. After all, on a hot day, a can of cold Coke is more highly prized that on a windy, wet cold day. People found this unfair.

If the announcement had stated instead that the price would go down with cooler weather (starting, of course, with a higher price as the norm), then no one would have been upset.

No customer gets upset about price decreases.

Using the Price Structure to Motivate Sales Staff

"If you want people motivated to do a good job, give them a good job to do." — Frederick Herzberg[38]

Pricing has a strong bearing on how to pay sales staff and what commission to offer. "Only sales incentive plans that abundantly reward above-average price realization and deeply penalize below average price levels will draw smart and profitable transaction price management from the sales force."[39]

Many years ago I operated an installation company in Vancouver. The installers pressured the company to pay them a commission on the parts used. This was a practice employed by 50 percent of the companies in the area to keep their fixed costs low but with the variable costs always producing a profit.

Just paying a commission on sales, I knew, was a killer. It would be a low percentage and act as a demotivator. And they needed price flexibility to be able to manage cranky customers.

So I created a price list based on my costs, where the costs included raw costs, plus the carrying costs, plus my expected return on investment and overhead. This I presented as the cost, and gave three price levels above that for the price list.

TABLE 19
COST VERSUS PRICE

Product Cost	$ 2.00	
Carrying Cost	$ 1.50	
Total Costs	$ 3.50	
List Price	$ 7.00	
		$ 1.75
Optional Price 1	$ 6.00	
		$ 1.25
Optional Price 2	$ 5.50	
		$ 1.00

List price generated a commission ($7.00 − ($2.00 + $1.50)) = $3.50/2 = $1.75

---

38. "Industry Week," No. 21, 1987. quoted in the *Oxford Book of Phrases, Sayings and Quotations*
39. Michael V. Marn and Robert L. Rosiello. "Managing price, gaining Profit." Harvard Business Review. Sept-Oct. 1992

The difference between my cost and the price charged to the client was split 50/50 with the technicians. 50 percent commission is a great motivator and because of the way it was set up, they could never sell below a price where I made money.

Moreover, I had a policy that should anyone complain to me about pricing — take it up with the boss — we would return 100 percent of the price charged if the customer bought a replacement for me somewhere else, at a cheaper price and brought it to the store. Not once did anyone do that.

Responding to a Price War

So the other cabinet maker in town suddenly and dramatically lowers prices. What do you do? Like gas stations, do you follow suit and match the price? The response that customers have to gas stations lowering the price of a fill-up is that if this is the price you can sell the stuff for, then they have been ripped off for months. Do you want your existing customers to think that you have been charging exorbitant rates for years just because you drop a price now?

To respond, it is best to know why your competitor has dropped his or her price. Do they have a warehouse full of cabinets that are not moving? Is this a short-term response to financial needs? Does he or she have a trailer load of substandard or damaged goods to move out?

Let us suppose that this is a grab for larger market share. How do you respond and keep your credibility? Is your service demonstrably better? Are your delivery times better? Is your service order backlog smaller? Do you have a product line that has unique items or extras that the competitor cannot match?

Before considering lowering prices, go back to Chapter 4 and re-evaluate your Unique Selling Proposition, and find the pressure points to fight back against lower prices.

What happens if you have to lower prices? Make absolutely certain that the minute your competitor raises prices back to normal levels, that you follow suit. This preserves your profit margins and also signals to your competitor that you are watching and rewarding him or her for increasing prices.

Summary

In this chapter, we looked at the consequences of pricing decisions. The responses to pricing decisions come from customers and from marketing and sales. This is where the rubber hits the road and like any other business decision, the consequences have to be anticipated, measured, and then countered.

When anticipating responses to pricing decisions, we discussed linking value to the price structure, training staff to deal with sticker shock, examining the likelihood of customers leaving, and looking at the possibility of price discrimination as a strategy to get full value.

We explored price discrimination and the business opportunity it represents. We looked at the ideas behind pocket price banding that help segment the customer population by what they buy at what price.

Bundling and unbundling are really merchandising concepts that provide imaginative solutions in pricing decisions by lumping together poor performers and great performers.

In contracting, or any type of business, it is important to realize that a price that is too low means all jobs can come your way — the winner's curse. Therefore, we have to learn to lose a percentage of sales.

We explored the mechanics of selling from the best to the least by selling best, better, good. Since staff motivation is always important, price can be used to motivate sales staff.

Finally, we covered what to do in the event of a price war.

8
PRICING MODELS

Previously this book has focused on costs, but in this chapter, we will explore pricing models typically employed by manufacturers that are also adaptable to other industries.

By this part of the book you will be aware that price is only part of the game of selling your product or service. In the salesperson's armory are credit terms, delivery schedules and return policies, to name three in a myriad of factors that influence a buyer.

We also have to give a nod to quality and flexibility. These apply particularly to manufacturers but have applications in other sectors. Quality and zero-defect policies affect price. If your product is known to be substandard, you will never be able to get a premium price unless you are dealing with a rookie purchaser. It's likely that purchaser will only buy once.

Flexibility refers to the ability of the firm to deliver a wide range of products on short timelines. If you can do that, buyers will love you and price will become a secondary issue.

Let us assume for the moment that your cost-cutting and constraint-removing programs are well underway. What type of pricing can you best use? First, let's consider the concept of capacity utilization.

Influence of Capacity Utilisation

"Capacity utilisation" is a concept in economics typically expressed as a percentage or ration. It measures the extent to which an enterprise actually uses its installed productive capacity. Usually it refers to capital goods like machinery. The ratio measures the relationship between actual output produced and potential output at full utilization of machinery.

In general, if market demand grows, capacity utilization will rise, and conversely, if demand weakens, capacity utilization will slacken. Economists and bankers closely watch capacity utilization indicators for signs of inflation pressures.

There is a common belief that when utilization rises above somewhere between 82 percent and 85 percent, price inflation will increase. On the other hand, excess capacity means that insufficient demand exists to warrant expansion of output.

There is substantial statistical and anecdotal evidence that many industries in the developed capitalist economies suffer from chronic excess capacity. Critics of market capitalism argue that the system is not as efficient as it may seem, since at least 20 percent more output could be produced and sold, if buying power was better distributed. However, a level of utilization somewhat below the maximum normally prevails, regardless of economic conditions.

In economic statistics, capacity utilization is normally surveyed for goods-producing industries at plant level. The results are presented as an average percentage rate by industry, and economy-wide, where 100 percent denotes full capacity. This rate is also sometimes called the "operating rate." If the operating rate is high, this is called "excess capacity," "surplus capacity," or "over capacity." The observed rates are often turned into indexes.

There has been some debate among economists about the validity of statistical measures of capacity utilization, because much depends on the survey questions asked, and on the valuation principles used to measure output. Also, the efficiency of production may change over time, due to new technologies.

Engineering and economic measures

One of the most used definitions of the "capacity utilization rate" is the ratio of actual output to the potential output. But potential output can be defined in at least two different ways.

One is the "engineering" or "technical" definition, according to which potential output represents the maximum amount of output that can be produced in the short-run with the existing stock. Thus, a standard definition of capacity utilization is the (weighted) average of the ratio between the actual output of firms to the maximum that could be produced per unit of time, with existing plant and equipment. Obviously, output could be measured in physical units or in market values, but normally it is measured in market values.

However, as output increases and well before the absolute physical limit of production is reached, most firms might well experience an increase in the average cost of production (even if there is no change in the level of plant and equipment used). For example, higher average costs can arise, because of the need to operate extra shifts, undertake additional plant maintenance, and so on.

An alternative approach, sometimes called the "economic utilization rate," is to measure the ratio of actual output to the estimated level of output, beyond which the average cost of production begins to rise. In this case, surveyed firms are asked by how much it would be practical for them to raise production from existing plant and equipment, without raising unit costs. Typically, this measure will yield a rate around 10 percentage points higher than the engineering measure, but will show the same movement over time.

Output gap measure

As a derivative indicator, the output gap (percentage OG) percentage can be measured as actual output (AO) less potential output (PO) divided by potential output x 100 = (AO/PO-1) x 100.

Executives will also let capacity utilization play a devastating psychological game with their pricing, especially when it is underutilized. The logic seems to be "better to do some job at low cost than no job at all," despite the potential for very serious long-run consequences, such as sending a message into the market that your firm will surrender on price, thereby degrading the integrity of your pricing. It also rewards your customers for shopping on price, a practice they will continue unabated until forced to make a value trade-off.

Worse, as found in a study[40] by Claudio Castelo Branco Puty, in the Department of Economics, Universidade Federal do Pará in Brazil, when demand falls, businesses hoard labour — keep their trained and valuable employees — in anticipation of an upswing in demand. While in his study the relationship between cost of materials and capacity marched in lock step, the unit wage costs of labour were largely inelastic compared to plant capacity. Where companies behave this way, prices cannot move downward quickly and keep a decent profit margin. The cost structure is warped away from the pure model of statistical curves to predict pricing.

On the upside, capacity utilization can present some interesting business opportunities. Printingforless.com is a business that matches demand with idle printing presses. Since an average $5 million Heidelberg press sits idle for most of its life, this is a great deal for the customer and a profit opportunity for the press owner. Since the transaction is blind, the press owner's regular pricing is not affected.

Similarly there are companies exploiting downtime in fully automated milling machines in the United States. Since these types of machines can be loaded before quitting time and then left in the cold and darkened machine shop to churn out widgets, the profit stream is above and beyond what was normally received for daytime jobs. The price typically reflects this use of the marginal costs of running machines after hours since the fixed costs are paid and the variable costs are the raw materials and power.

New Product Introduction

When a new product enters the market, the company and its marketing team have a choice of market skimming, also known as skim pricing, penetration pricing, or neutral pricing. This decision is important because in the absence of any experience with a brand new product, the price tells the potential customer what value the company places on their new offering.

According to Michael Marn, a McKinsey & Company consultant, "When a new product pricing error is made, 80 to 90 percent of the time the release price is too low. Release price, also launch or target price, is the price you want the market to associate with that

---

40. "Cost Curves and Capacity Utilization in U.S. Manufacturing, 1958-1996." Claudio Castelo Branco Puty, Department of Economics, Universidade Federal do Pará

product. More than any press release, sales pitch, or catalog description, the price tells the market what a company really thinks a new product is worth."[41]

Market Skimming

In market skimming, the prices are initially set high to "skim" revenue layer by layer from the market. It works best when:

- Quality and image support the higher price.

- Enough buyers want the product at that price.

- Cost of producing a small volume cannot be high.

- Competitors should not be able to enter the market easily.

Rather than introduce a product or service at a single set price, the price slowly slides downward as each layer of the market segment is exploited then expanded to include the next layer. The early adopters are the ones paying the highest price for being the first with the latest gadget.

Price is sometimes seen as an indicator of quality. Take for example the price of wine versus the price of gasoline. Shifting the price of gasoline upwards will not have customers queuing up to buy that "extra-special fuel." In fact, we as consumers expect that gasoline from any pump will be basically identical to all the others. Having a highly-priced bottle of wine, on the other hand, is a mark of value.

Take the instance of a new gadget entering the market. For a portion of the population, at least, having the latest gadget with full knowledge of the fact that within a year or two, the price will fall dramatically, is important. These are the early adapters. Bragging rights are the early adapters' only concern. The first VCRs sold between 1963 and 1968 sold for $30,000 at Neiman Marcus.

In both instances, there is a tiny cross-section of the target market that is willing to pay for the perceived value of the fine bottle of wine or the newest gadget. Price is not the major factor in these buying decisions.

The pricing decisions made here assume that the initial target market is not too tiny and that the cost of production for a small number is not prohibitive.

---

41. Michael Marn et. al. The Price Advantage. quoted in Baker. Ronald J. Pricing on Purpose. Creating and Capturing Value. John Wiley and Sons Inc. Hoboken, New Jersey. 2006 p. 29

After the initial offerings at a high price and after sales have slowed, the price can drop to the next layer where the company has determined there is another segment of the population who will buy. It may take decades and dozens of price drops to reach the point where VCRs were a few years ago, when they were being sold at rock-bottom prices by all the chain stores.

There is an assumption here that it is difficult for competitors to enter the market quickly to undercut your price on an initial offering. With a brand new product, it will take time for competitors to make a reasonable facsimile. During that honeymoon period when you have the only gadget on the market, you have the upper hand.

How much more profit will there be in this type of pricing strategy? Consider the two tables below. In this market, the company has determined that the final total of items that can be sold into the market is 6,000, and that costs are $30. If the company sells all its items at $60 then the margin will be $210,000.

TABLE 20
BRAND NEW PRODUCT

Cost	Selling Price	Margin	Quantity	Total Profit Opportunity
$ 30	$ 65	$ 35	6000	$ 210,000

TABLE 21
SELLING ALL 6,000 UNITS AT $35 PROFIT MARGIN

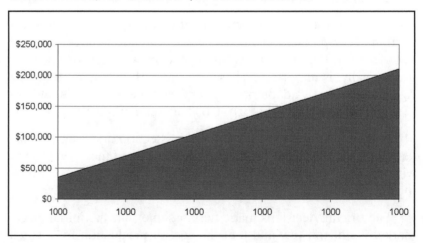

If, however, this company layers the pricing to sell the first release at $250, then $175, then $115, and finally $65 to capture all of
the 6,000 possible sales, then the profit margin is $465,000, or over
twice the increase in profit.

TABLE 22
LAYERED PRICING

Cost	Selling Price	Margin	Quantity	Total Profit Opportunity
$ 30	$ 250	$ 220	500	$ 110,000
$ 30	$ 175	$ 145	750	$ 108,750
$ 30	$ 115	$ 85	1000	$ 85,000
$ 30	$ 85	$ 85	1500	$ 82,500
$ 30	$ 65	$ 35	2250	$ 78,750
			6000	$ 465,000

TABLE 23
MARGIN DOLLARS EARNED WITH LAYERED PRICING

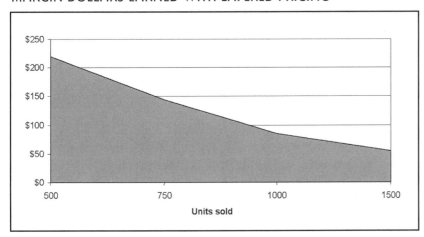

Penetration Pricing

Penetration pricing is used deliberately to set prices below the customer's perceived value in order to secure a large and immediate
market share.

The danger with penetration pricing, of course, is to let your competitors influence your pricing too heavily. That would be in the interests of your competitors', not your company's, financial future.

This strategy was used by Lexus, which entered the market at a
price 40 percent below the Mercedes and BMW markets it targeted.

This was also the strategy employed by Mazda when it introduced the Miata model to gain a foothold in the sports car market.

Penetration pricing can be used where:

- Demand for the product is elastic (a drop in price will mean more sales).

- The product's value can easily be judged by the customer immediately after use.

- The threat of competitor imitation of your product or service is strong.

- There is a large portion of eager wannabe-buyers who cannot buy at the higher price and your pricing strategy will get them to the table.

- You have the capacity and financial backing to produce the volumes needed.

- Your low introductory price may prevent competitors from entering the market and competing for a while.[42]

For penetration marketing to succeed, competitors must not be able to follow the price cut easily. Only where competitors lack the ability or incentive to follow is it practical. There are three common situations where this is likely to occur:

1. "When the firm has a significant cost advantage and/or resource advantage so that its competitors believe they would lose if they began a price war.

2. When the firm has a broader line of complementary products, enabling it to use one as a penetration-priced 'loss leader' in order to drive sales of others.

3. When the firm is currently so small that it can significantly increase its sales without affecting the sales of its competitors enough to prompt a response."[43]

Penetration pricing is typically used after a solid market segment has been established. The examples above are from well-established market brands where it is unnecessary to convince customers of the quality or reputation of the manufacturer.

42. Baker. Ronald J. *Pricing on Purpose. Creating and Capturing Value.* John Wiley and Sons Inc. Hoboken, New Jersey. 2006, p 233

43. Nagle, Thomas T., Hogan, John, *Strategy and Tactics of Pricing: Guide to Grow More Profitably,* 4th edition, 2006. Reprinted by permission of Pearson Education Inc., Upper Saddle River, NJ

Beware: Penetration prices are deliberately set relative to the value of the product in the marketplace. Do not let your competitors set the price. They, after all, are not interested in the long term viability of your company.

Neutral Pricing

Neutral pricing, as its name may imply, means that price is not the largest factor in determining a sales strategy. In fact, in neutral pricing, sales will take place because emphasis is given in the marketing of the product to value-added aspects of the product or company. It may be delivery times, carrying inventory for the buyer, offering credit terms, maintenance contracts, regular free updates, or ongoing and supportive relationships. These powerful advantages mean that there is no price differentiation in the marketplace.

Activity-Based Costing (ABC) and Pricing

Traditionally, cost accountants arbitrarily added a broad percentage onto the direct costs (materials and labor, etc.) to allow for the indirect (freight, taxes, etc.) costs.

However, as the percentages of overhead costs rise, this technique becomes increasingly inaccurate because the indirect costs are not caused equally by all the products. For example, one product might take more time in one expensive machine than another product, but since the amount of direct labor and materials might be the same, the additional cost for the use of the machine would not be recognised when the same broad "on-cost" percentage is added to all products. Consequently, when multiple products share common costs, there is a danger of one product subsidising another.

The concepts of ABC were developed in the manufacturing sector of the United States during the 1970s and 1980s. During this time, the Consortium for Advanced Manufacturing-International, now known simply as CAM-I, provided a formative role for studying and formalizing the principles that have become more formally known as Activity-Based Costing.

Instead of using arbitrary percentages to allocate costs, ABC seeks to identify cause and effect relationships to assign costs objectively. Once the costs of the activities have been identified, the cost of each activity can be attributed to each product to the extent that the product uses the activity. In this way ABC often identifies areas of high overhead costs per unit and so directs attention to finding ways to reduce the costs or to charge more for costly products.

Like manufacturing industries, financial institutions also have diverse products which can cause cross-product subsidies. Since personnel expenses represent the largest single component of non-interest expenses in financial institutions, these costs must also be attributed more accurately to products and customers. Activity-based costing, even though developed for manufacturing, can be a useful tool for doing this.

Direct labor and materials are relatively easy to trace directly to products, but it is more difficult to directly allocate indirect costs to products. Where products use common resources differently, some sort of weighting is needed in the cost-allocation process. The measure of the use of a shared activity by each of the products is known as the cost-driver. For example, the cost of the activity of bank tellers can be assigned to each product by measuring how long each product's transaction takes at the counter and then by measuring the number of each type of transaction.

Three things can happen when establishing product prices. If a price is set too high, it could result in a lost sale that could have been profitable at a lower price. If a price is set too low, then all of your work isn't as profitable. Only when a price is set appropriately does a company make both a sale and a profit. Just as activity-based costing and activity-based management revolutionized the cost accounting world, activity-based pricing brings a disciplined approach to developing pricing. Activity-based pricing examines the relationships between price, cost and sales volume and how this relationship affects profitability.

Gary Cokins noted in his essay, "Are All of Your Customers Profitable?"[44] that some customers purchase a mix of relatively low-price and low-margin products. When you consider the costs-to-serve those customers as distinct from the original cost of the widget or service you sold, these customers may be unprofitable. It just costs so much to look after them.

Here are some questions you need to answer about your products and customers.

• Do we push for volume or margin with specific customers?

---

44. Cokins, Gary. Are All of Your Customers Profitable? A Technical bulletin from ABC Technologies. Beaverton, Oregon. 1999

- Are there ways to improve profitability by altering the package of products or services we sell?

- Does the sales volume justify the discounts we give?

- Can we change customers to our new profit-directed strategy?

Limitations of ABC

Even in activity-based costing, some overhead costs are difficult to assign to products and customers, for example the chief executive's salary. These costs are termed "business sustaining" and are not assigned to products and customers because there is no meaningful method to do so. This lump of unallocated overhead costs must nevertheless be met by contributions from each of the products, but it is not as large as the overhead costs before ABC is employed.

Marginal Cost Pricing

In economics and finance, marginal cost is the change in total cost that arises when the quantity produced changes by one unit.

TABLE 24
A TYPICAL MARGINAL COST CURVE

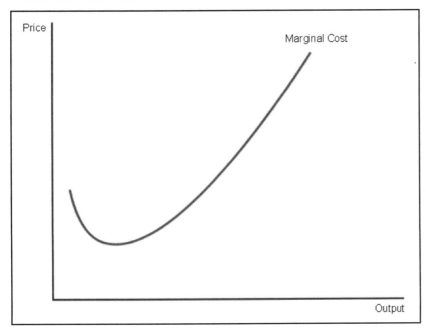

Basically, marginal cost at each level of production includes any additional costs needed to produce the next unit. For example, if a bakery aims to produce a higher volume of bread to accommodate increased demand, the marginal cost of that increased production includes the cost of new equipment and extra labor. At each stage of production over a given time period, marginal costs include all those costs which are variable at the point of production. Other costs are considered fixed costs, which, by definition, do not change with production volume.

The principle of marginal cost pricing is that the market will inevitably drive goods to be sold at their marginal cost of production. Outside factors, such as competition and market demand, will affect whether goods are actually sold at their marginal cost. Marginal cost equals marginal revenue, so market price will be determined according to current supply and demand, and a producer should aim to produce and sell where his or her marginal cost is less than the current market price. Therefore, to make a profit, the marginal cost of producing a higher volume of bread should be less per unit than the salable price per loaf.

Economies of scale, a concept in which an increase in the scale of a company causes a decrease in the long term average cost of each unit, exist when marginal cost falls to a point where it is less than the average cost per unit, the point where your marginal costs equal your marginal revenues. Production may be subject to economies of scale, or, conversely, diseconomies of scale (wherein a company grows beyond the scale of production that minimizes long-run average cost, such as where the size of the market does not allow for maximized profit, or where there is limited consumer demand).

I have mentioned the technical definitions here because they have been discussed so often in the boardrooms of manufacturers. It leads to pricing decisions to get the price low enough to entice a customer to place a really large order. However, it is not necessarily the way to get the biggest margins and the biggest profits.

There are times when marginal pricing should be avoided.

Never do it if:

- It can possibly create a precedent in the long run with your big customers. Marginal pricing is by its very nature not sustainable in the medium and long term.

- The news of your spectacular price can reach the marketplace and alert other customers that better prices can be achieved.

- It commits you to extra capital cost in the short or the long run. If you have to buy new machines to get a marginal-priced product out of the door, you cannot hope to pay for the machines out of cash flow.

- Marginal pricing deals consume resources needed elsewhere in the organization. All this entails is that you will be stripping resources always from deals that are profitable to finance and support a deal that is not by its nature profitable.

- You have to sacrifice some full-profit deal to fit in the marginal-priced deal.

- It costs you cash flow as well. A great deal on a price should always be attached to an agreement to pay up front or upon receipt.

- It undermines your company's market position.

With a little creativity and attention to what adds value for your customers, marginal pricing can be used against your competition. In his fictional account of a printing company competing for candy wrapper orders[45], Eliyahu Goldratt explores a standard printing industry problem. As quantities rise, the fixed cost of the set-up diminishes and the price drops. Everyone knows that. So how does the little guy compete with the giants and their fast printing machinery?

You could drop prices if there is excess plant capacity. On the last few orders run through the plant and with all fixed costs covered and only the raw material costs to take into account, any price above variable costs is profit. Therefore it should be possible to compete on a limited number of small-run print jobs. But it still leaves money on the table.

However, what if you cannot utilize that excess capacity? Taking on a job at prices to match the competitors would have a disastrous impact on your bottom line. So, could you just price match and hope to win the order due to your charming personality alone?

Goldratt goes on to explain why it is risky to match competitors' prices for his printer story. The same clients who order large quantities of wrappers for the popular candies are ordering smaller

45. Eliyahu M. Goldratt. *It's Not Luck*. North River Press. Barrington, MA (1994) p 66-70

quantities for the less popular candies. Therefore the buyers expect that the larger the volume, the lower the price per unit. If the printing plant reduces price per unit on the large quantities, the buyer will demand a proportional reduction on the small quantities, even if for those quantities you currently offer lower prices than the competition.

The ingrained behaviour of the buyers would create pressure to lower prices across the board and that could ruin the industry.

But what if profitability was only one of the financial indicators that the potential purchaser was working towards? There is another one, which sometimes is even more important than profit — cash flow. And a good salesperson will be able to bring back information on a client to find this sweet spot. Cash flow is a major concern for some customers. So does knowing this fact convince them to pay higher prices?

Ordering more frequently, in smaller quantities, ties up less cash in inventory. Even if the buyer has to pay higher prices for small orders, his or her company is much better off by accepting smaller demands on cash flow. And when cash flow is pressing, only short-term considerations exist.

Suppose that cash flow is not the constraint? Goldratt goes on to explain that the printing company could mount a direct attack on the assumption that ordering in large quantities gives the buyer a cheaper price-per-unit. In the fictional printing company the plant manager triumphantly points out that the order they just lost to a low cost, high volume producer would in fact be a quantity that represents the buyer's needs for the next six months. So what?

In this example, the plant manager has researched the industry, and found some statistics from an industry trade magazine that showed product obsolescence timelines. He found that his customer's forecast was becoming more unreliable as the time frames enlarged. The customer's own push for more and more marketing campaigns caused them to change, much more frequently, some of the printing on the wrappers. So a six-month order of candy wrappers had only a 30 percent chance of being completely used.

The solution in this story was that the chance of not using the entire quantity before it was made obsolete by a new sales campaign was much less when the order was only enough to cover the next two months. All that had to be done was to convince the client to consider product obsolescence, as the client should, when ordering in batches of two months. This gives him or her an effective cheaper price-per-unit than ordering in batches of six months from the competitors. After all, when you divide the entire cost of a six month order quantity by the number of wrappers they can reasonably expect to use, the price per unit will increase.

Goldratt's fictional plant manager sees the new approach unfolding; to sell a valuable benefit to his customer. The buyer will not consider the purchased price-per-unit, but rather the price he or she paid per unit likely to be used.

I have discussed this story at length because it takes a seemingly hard-to-manage problem faced every day, by the owners of businesses large and small. When confronted by the loss of an order and considering the next quote, how can you get the price low enough to get that job but still create a profit? In the example, the business owner found value for the customer by identifying the value in having fewer unused printed wrappers made obsolete by changes in the customer's marketing plan. Smaller orders meant that this fictional printer with its smaller machines and shorter setup times had lower fixed costs. Larger firms with larger machines could not follow and compete with this small printer.

Summary

In this chapter we considered six types of pricing structures utilized by small manufacturers: the influence of capacity utilization; market skimming; neutral pricing; penetration pricing; activity-based costing and pricing; and marginal pricing. Each type of pricing has its uses and its downfalls. Next, we'll look at financial analysis for your business.

9
FINANCIAL ANALYSIS

The purpose of this chapter is to provide the tools for simple price analysis and to help you perform some "what-if" calculations.

To begin, we examine costs, because I have met so many business owners who do not have a firm grasp of their job costing, product costs, or labor costs. Even with all the emphasis on value pricing in this book, costs are the foundation on which prices are built. Having mastered that, the business owner can use the simple math tools that will enable him or her to make a judgment about whether to increase or drop prices.

From that point on, there is a natural progression to my favorite way of looking at businesses — from the goal (profit, presumably) to the means of achieving that goal. This is frequently called predetermined profitability, and is built on the assumption that a business exists to generate profit.

Know Your Real Costs: Labor
What is the real cost of labor?

Too often small business owners appear oblivious to the real cost of labor and respond to my enquiries that the $12 per hour they pay to their employee, Joe, is the cost of labor.

Joe works for $12 per hour, yes. But he also takes paid vacations as per labor laws.

Joe lives and works in Canada, so he also contributes to Employment Insurance and Canada Pension Plan (CPP), to which the company contributes a similar portion.

Joe might also have a benefit package for glasses, dental work, and extended health benefits.

Joe is also covered by accident insurance against work-related injuries by the old Worker's Compensation Board in British Columbia, now WorkSafeBC, for which the employer pays.

TABLE 25
LABOR COST EXAMPLE

	Employee Labor Cost (per hour)
Labor Rate	$ 12.00
Vacation pay (4 percent, 2 weeks per year)	$ 0.48
Employer Portion of Employment Insurance	$ 0.50
Employer Portion of CPP or similar plan	$ 0.50
Benefits — 12 percent	$ 1.44
WCB – dependent upon the industry	$ 0.25
Total Labor Cost	$ 15.17

In this little example, the original cost of labor has climbed past the nominal $12.00 per hour to $15.17 per hour because of payroll taxes. This is 25 percent more than the owner believes costs to be. Typically, 25 percent as the payroll tax markup is a great rule of thumb but this needs to be worked out in detail for each company.

Why is this important? Suppose you are quoting labor rates for your cleaning business and you base your profit expectation on paying Joe $12 per hour as per the chart below. You look for a contribution to overheads and the owner's paycheck of $6 per hour. If you add 50 percent to Joe's rate, selling his labor at $18, you think you stand to make $6 per hour of profit, or 33 percent.

TABLE 26
PAYROLL TAXES AS PART OF LABOR COST

Joes Hourly Wage	$12.00		Joe's Hourly Wage	$12.00	
			Payroll Taxes @ 25 percent	$ 3.17	
Markup @ 50 percent	$ 6.00		Total Cost per Hour	$15.17	
Selling Price Per Hour	$18.00		Selling Price per Hour	$18.00	
Anticipated Profit	$ 6.00	33 percent	Actual Profit	$ 2.83	16 percent

The reality is that the payroll taxes eat up $3.17 per hour, halving the profit to $2.83 or a measly 16 percent. Profit is still being made on each job but the contribution level (pricing) means that the business slowly starves to death.

There is another area frequently forgotten in costing, and that is downtime. Each employee is entitled to coffee breaks. If you are manufacturing, there is always downtime while that elusive micrometer is found. If you are a service company with technicians driving to peoples' homes, there is the travel time during which no work is being done. These add to your costs even though you don't really write a check to cover them. They get buried in your payroll costs.

While some of these costs are inevitable, some are avoidable. Lean manufacturing techniques focus on the time taken for setting up machines. In the late 1980s the big US auto manufacturers were taking 3 weeks to re-tool a line to switch to another production model. The Japanese auto makers could make that switch in 24 hours. The impact was that if model X was not selling and the car lots were full of unsold models, the nimbler Japanese could switch to producing a better-selling model much quicker by comparison. The US manufacturers, meanwhile, would continue to fill car lots with unsold cars. Then the prices would have to be dropped to move out these unsold vehicles.

Know Your Real Costs: Product

Is the cost of that shovel the dollar amount indicated on the invoice from the distributor?

What about freight costs?

What about the cost of purchasing, handling, unpacking, and warehousing that shovel until it is sold?

What about financing costs? Are you using your bank overdraft at 10 percent to pay that invoice in 30 days to keep your account in good standing, while it may be 60 days before you get paid?

Many companies do a spectacular job of assigning even the tiniest costs of the company to individual items in order to reap enough profit to pay for everything.

This is cost-up pricing and should be the baseline upon which you make pricing decisions. After all, being creative with prices does not allow you to sell below your costs.

> Example: In the 1980s my salesman came with an order for Wallaceburg plumbing spindles. They were no longer made and all the inventory had disappeared. Nevertheless, I found a firm willing to make them but with a minimum order of 100. However, the salesman had 2 orders totaling 25 spindles. I realized that I would buy 100 and sell 25 leaving me with 75 probably unsalable spindles. I was determined that I would not be out of pocket on this transaction, so I priced them to cover the invoice cost, handling costs, and sales commission for the entire order. So, if the cost was $12 each at invoice price, and handling and commissions added $3, and my profit expectation was $5, the total bill would be $2,000 (100 x (12 + 3 +5)). The charge for 25 spindles would be $2,000 so that if I sold 25 or the entire amount, I would make a profit and not grimace every time I counted the unsold spindles in my inventory.

Know Your Real Costs: Overheads

In the appendices, I recommend that you organize your profit and loss statements so that direct costs — material and labor — are placed immediately below gross sales and that the net is your gross margin. This is to help the business owner focus on gross margin.

In Table 27, it looks like the gross margin is a healthy 83 percent which could lead your marketing department to believe that price can be more flexible and to start offering price discounts.

TABLE 27
OVERHEAD COSTS

Net Sales	$100,000	100 percent
DIRECT COSTS		
Cost of Goods Sold	$ 17,000	17 percent
GROSS PROFIT	$ 83,000	83 percent
Sales and G&A Expenses		
Advertising and Promotion	$ 3,000	3 percent
Direct Labor	$ 43,000	43 percent
Direct of Subcontractor	$ 2,000	2 percent
Other Direct Expenses	$ 6,700	7 percent
Depreciation	$ 689	1 percent
Facilities Expenses	$ 2,800	3 percent
Interest Expenses	$ 125	0 percent
Officers' Compensation	$ 7,500	8 percent
Salaries and Commissions	$ 3,400	3 percent
Other Salaries/Commissions	$ 2,000	2 percent
Other Sales Expenses	$ 4,589	5 percent
Other G&A Expenses	$ 500	1 percent
TOTAL SALES G&A Expenses	$ 76,303	76 percent
Net Operating Profit	$ 6,697	7 percent

But it also helps to know what your overheads are. These are not necessarily the same as fixed costs but often they are fixed in that they cannot easily be changed. Rent and utilities cannot change very much but advertising can be killed off completely in a cash crunch. Overheads are also the things you pay for in an organization that you do not directly charge for. For example, no one that I'm aware of has ever added advertising costs directly to an invoice.

Overhead costs drive pricing with a force equal to direct costs but it is more subtle. If, to return a previous example, Joe's labor rate is $12 plus payroll taxes, but the cost of all the overheads amounts to (but not including profit) another $4.25 per hour then the real cost is $12 + $3 + $4.25.

Know Your Real Costs: Debt

Debt is a fixed cost because you have likely agreed through a lease or a mortgage to a fixed payment every month for a specified number of months or years. Even if the business has a bad six months, the rent or mortgage payments still have to be made.

From a pricing perspective, having tons of debt limits the flexibility of the business to reduce prices in the face of fierce competition.

When you total the cost of material and the true cost of labor and the absolutely-must-pay fixed costs, then divide that by the number of hours you bill or the number of widgets you make, you have cost. But if your debt load is really high, even the cost of serving that debt will suck vital cash out of the business.

This not to say that all debt is bad. It just limits the capacity of the business to open up new markets with aggressive pricing, take advantage of suppliers' price offers or to increase inventory in the knowledge of forthcoming shortages. Cash is king.

Most business owners would like to own the building from which they conduct their business. Even though sophisticated financial analysis shows that it is better to rent and take the difference between mortgage payments and the rent and invest that money, the reality is different. Paying a mortgage every month is a savings plan. If it is a building and land that is being purchased, it will presumably increase in value just as you decrease the debt. And in the event that you have found no other way to produce a retirement nest egg, the building satisfies that requirement very nicely.

Know Your Real Costs: Transaction Costs

Transaction costs eat up profits. There are many different kinds of transactions with attached costs:

- prompt payment discounts offered to customers to accelerate the cash flow,

- volume buying incentives,

- cooperative advertising allowances,

- free deliver,

- one year unlimited help line access, and

- six months extra parts and labor warranty to Company BCV.

This is the so-called Pocket Price Waterfall. "The manufacturer offered a series of discounts and incentives that affected its product's pocket price. The company gave dealers a 2 percent payment terms discount if they paid an invoice within 30 days. It offered an annual volume bonus of up to 5 percent based on a dealer's total purchases. Retailers received cooperative advertising allowances of up to 4 percent if they featured the manufacturer's products in their advertising. And the company paid freight for transporting goods to the retailer on all orders exceeding a certain dollar value. Taken individually, none of these offerings significantly affected profit. Together, however, they amounted to a 22.7 percent difference between the invoice and pocket prices."[46]

Is your company suffering from poor margins because of these transaction costs?

After you have examined your company's pricing and transaction costs, flip this picture on its head. If your suppliers are offering any of the above, does your company take full advantage of them? For example, a 2 percent discount on early payment of an invoice means that 2 percent will drop to the bottom line and add measurably to your profit picture. Yes, this is cost cutting, but each dollar on the bottom line gives you more flexibility when faced with stiff price competition. Companies with really slender bottom lines have no price flexibility.

"Even if a company's managers make the right pricing decisions 90 percent of the time, it's worthwhile to try for 92 percent — the payoff is that high. But the price lever is a double-edged sword ... a mere 1 percent price decrease for an average company, for instance, would destroy 11.1 percent of the company's operating profit."[47]

The Impact of Discounting Prices
Calculating how many extra sales are needed to offset a price decrease

In most companies, there is a daily battle between the salespeople who wish to hit their quotas by having a rock bottom price, and the accounting people who see lost profits. In smaller companies, this struggle takes place in the mind of the single owner.

---

46. Michael V. Marn and Robert L. Rosiello. "Managing price, gaining Profit." Harvard Business Review. Sept-Oct. 1992

47. Michael V. Marn and Robert L. Rosiello. "Managing price, gaining Profit." Harvard Business Review. Sept-Oct. 1992

There are three scenarios for this price volume trade-off.

1. With no change to variable or fixed cost
2. With a change to variable cost only
3. With a change to fixed cost only

With no change to variable or fixed cost

Most price decreases are undertaken based on the assumption that a price drop will generate huge sales and therefore huge profits. Table 28 shows how to calculate what sales volume is required to offset this decrease and to help set targets for sales staff. The actual math can be found in Appendix II.

> OLDCO Company is considering a 5 percent price cut on its buckets of dog biscuits, which will change the price from $9.95 to $9.45 and thus make the company more competitive within its trading area. Marketing believes that they will be able to sell 20 percent more. The operations manager believes that variable costs will not have to change in response to this pricing decision — i.e., that the company will not have to look for cheaper raw materials.

In Table 28, the price effect shows that a price decrease on each bucket will reduce corporate profits by $5,000 to $25,000. In order to recoup these losses the volume must increase to 11,268 or 11.27 percent — just to keep even. If marketing is correct in its estimates, then a price decrease should generate a larger volume of buckets sold and more profit.

TABLE 28
IMPACT OF A PRICE DECREASE

	Now	Price Effect	New Volumes Required
Sales in Units	10,000	10,000	11,268
Price per Unit	$ 9.95	$ 9.45	$ 9.45
Revenue Total	$ 99,500.00	$ 94,500.00	$ 106,479.00
Variable Costs per Unit	$ 5.45	$ 5.45	$ 5.45
Gross Margin per Unit	$ 4.50	$ 4.00	$ 4.00
Total Gross Margin	$ 45,000.00	$ 40,000.00	$ 45,070.00
Fixed Costs	$ 15,000.00	$ 15,000.00	$ 15,000.00
Profit	$ 30,000.00	$ 25,000.00	$ 30,070.00

So, if marketing is correct and OLDCO can sell 20 percent more buckets of dog biscuits, profit will jump by $3,000.

With a change to variable cost only

In this example we have left fixed costs alone and allowed for a change in variable costs and price only in order to reflect a declining cost of production or, in the case of distributor or retailer, a drop in unit price due to a larger commitment. In this instance, the cost to make or buy a unit will drop the more you buy, or the more you make. In this company's marketing plan, price decreases are undertaken on the assumption that a price drop will generate a temporary drop in margins followed by huge sales and therefore huge profits. Table 29 will show the business owner how to calculate what sales volume is required to offset this decrease and to help him or her set targets for sales staff.

TABLE 29
IMPACT OF PRICE DECREASE AND CHANGE IN VARIABLE COSTS

Change in Variable Costs Only	Now	Price Effect	Sales Needed
Sales in Units	10,000	10,000	11,268
Price per Unit	$ 9.95	$ 9.45	$ 9.45
Revenue Total	$ 99,500.00	$ 94,500.00	$ 101,247.00
Variable Costs per Unit	$ 5.45	$ 5.25	$ 5.25
Gross Margin per Unit	$ 4.50	$ 4.20	$ 4.20
Total Gross Margin	$ 45,000.00	$ 42,000.00	$ 44,998.80
Fixed Costs	$ 15,000.00	$ 15,000.00	$ 15,000.00
Profit	$ 30,000.00	$ 27,000.00	$ 29,999.00

In this chart, the price effect of reducing prices and reducing costs means a fall in profits by $3,000 to $27,000. In order to regain the profitability levels, the company must sell more buckets of dog biscuits.

But if marketing is correct and there is a potential market out there for 2,000 more buckets what would the profit picture look like? See Table 30.

TABLE 30
IMPACT OF INCREASED SALES

Sales in Units	12,000
Price per Unit	$ 9.45
Revenue Total	$ 113,400.00
Variable Costs per Unit	$ 5.25
Gross Margin per Unit	$ 4.20
Total Gross Margin	$ 50,400.00
Fixed Costs	$ 15,000.00
Profit	$ 35,400.00

With a change to fixed cost only

In some instances fixed costs can change too and that will affect the price and the sales volume needed to offset a price drop. As hinted at earlier in the discussion on capacity utilization, as a plant nears full capacity, costs can increase; overtime to meet tight deadlines, maintenance frequency increases, etc.

OLDCO Company is considering a 5 percent price cut which will change the price of its buckets of dog treats from $9.95 to $9.45. Marketing believes that they will be able to sell 20 percent more. The operations manager believes that costs can be cut but will have to hire one more invoicing agent to cope with the extra workload. Fixed costs therefore will rise by $2,000.

TABLE 31
COULD A PRICE DROP INCREASE SALES?

Change in Variable and Fixed Costs	Now	Price Effect	Sales Needed
Sales in Units	10,000	10,000	11,190
Price per Unit	$ 9.95	$ 9.45	$ 9.45
Revenue Total	$ 99,500.00	$ 94,500.00	$ 105,746.00
Variable Costs per Unit	$ 5.45	$ 5.25	$ 5.25
Gross Margin per Unit	$ 4.50	$ 4.20	$ 4.20
Total Gross Margin	$ 45,000.00	$ 42,000.00	$ 46,998.00
Fixed Costs	$ 15,000.00	$ 17,000.00	$ 17,000.00
Profit	$ 30,000.00	$ 25,000.00	$ 29,998.00

In this example, the price has dropped by 50 cents. The variable costs have dropped by 30 cents per bucket of dog biscuits. However, the new staff member salary will cut profits. In order to recoup the old profit numbers, the new sales target is 11,190.

And what if marketing is right about a sales potential of 12,000? What will the picture look like then?

TABLE 32
SALES POTENTIAL

Change in Variable Costs Only	
Sales in Units	12,000
Price per Unit	$ 9.45
Revenue Total	$ 113,400.00
Variable Costs per Unit	$ 5.25
Gross Margin per Unit	$ 4.20
Total Gross Margin	$ 50,400.00
Fixed Costs	$ 15,000.00
Profit	$ 35,400.00

Profit could climb to $35,400, probably prompting a call from the salespeople for greater commissions.

Goal Setting From the Top

As with so many aspects of life, starting with the goal and working backwards to the means of achieving that goal works with pricing too.

If you have satisfactorily determined what the market will bear for your product or service you can then go back to manufacturing or sales or service and determine just exactly which features and benefits you can afford to offer at that given price. This is not the normal way of conducting business and is an especially price-driven concept as opposed to the usual "here's my product, I think I'll try and sell it" approach.

What should you do instead?

1. Establish how much money is invested in the business and what return is required.

2. Establish what value your customers see in your company or product.

3. Establish competitor pricing.

4. What are your broad strategic objectives? (More market share?)

Consider the following familiar example about a typical home business that started with a hobby that produced a nice product, and then the owner tried to find a market for it.

Bob Jones had been taking lovely photographs and making them into posters for his friends and acquaintances for years. The walls of his home were plastered with exquisite posters that everyone admired when they came to visit. People would comment that his photos were spectacular compared to the pedestrian posters in the stores. Bob decided to finally take the plunge and start a small business.

The family financed the purchase of sufficient framing materials to produce a dozen samples. Bob spent dozens of hours in his workshop cutting frame material, backing the posters and mounting the final product. He had chosen the best pictures and was confident of great results.

Then he took his collection to a large shop that sold posters and paintings. The shop was part of a big chain and the manager explained that she would have to get permission from the head office in Toronto to purchase and sell Bob's pictures. Bob was learning the traumas of becoming a salesperson the hard way.

A little shop selling home furnishings was his next call. The owner loved the posters, exclaiming that his customers would love them too. "How much are they?" was the dreaded question. Bob worked out all of his costs and calculated that he can create six posters per week. He knew the cost of the photographs, the framing and backing materials, added a little profit and $10 an hour for the labour component. He told the shop owner the price and got out his order book.

"Oh, that is a bit more than I wanted to pay," replied the shop owner.

Bob then learned the pain of selling to professional buyers, because buyers always think that what they are paying is too much. However, Bob wanted the sale. So he dropped the price and the shop owner agreed to buy 20 posters. Bob bought a cheap bottle of champagne on the way home.

Within two months, Bob was flooded with orders and worked every night till 11:00 p.m. in his workshop. He couldn't get any help because no one was willing to work for $10 an hour. The shop ordering most of the posters was taking a long time to pay their invoices and Bob's bank account was in overdraft.

Bob discovered the final part of the salesperson's dilemma; the sale is never really made until the money is in the bank.

Within three months, Bob collapsed from exhaustion and the family shipped him off to Mexico to recuperate.

That is the wrong way to do it.

Now let us assume that at this stage you decide to help Bob's enterprise. You will want to restart it on a sound commercial basis. First you get the Yellow Pages and search out which stores in town will likely carry posters. Then you visit each store and make a long list of what they offer, what styles, what is different and in what price ranges the store sells. Finally, in each store you note the other items on sale and likely the type of client they are trying to attract. You talk to the shop owners and confirm your observations. Finally, you create some original ideas of your own that will help Bob create a product that is truly different in the marketplace. This is market research.

Then you take a look at some competitors' products, study a little of their company background. How do they make their posters, how do they sell them, are they profitable? You develop some special ideas of your own based upon what the competitors are not offering.

Next, it's time to work out a budget. If Product-Unique is the highest priced product, you figure that the company may sell 200 posters in year one. If Product-Better-Than-Average is a medium-priced product that is well made and appeals to the clientele, and you noted in your market research then perhaps it will sell 450. If Product-Priced-to-Sell is unique enough and well made, then the company will likely sell 800 with a small but bearable difference between the selling price and cost.

Finally, it is time to make a production plan. You will need a production plan that will show Bob how long he can afford to spend making each item, and how much he can afford to spend on material. Is there a way to save money on materials? Could he use a blend of cheap and expensive backing material? That should keep his unit costs down and allow a profit margin at the price you have chosen.

Here, the market and profit opportunity are identified first. Notice that price is determined by a thorough marketplace evaluation and not by costs. Costs are recalculated to meet profit objectives, working backwards from the price.

That is also the wrong way to do it.

Now let us assume that at this stage you decide to help your neighbor's enterprise. He wants to get it restarted on a sound commercial basis. You search out the shops that would most likely stock patchwork items. You note first what sells and at what price and where. You talk to the shopkeepers. You create some original ideas to make something different from the existing products.

Then you work out a budget showing what money might be earned from different items sold in varying quantities. You have a look at some competitors' products, study a little of their company background. How do they make things, how do they sell them, are they profitable? You develop some special ideas of your own based upon what the competitors are not offering. You have an idea of the price at which you and your partner will sell your chosen items. You will need a production plan that will show you how long you and your neighbor can afford to spend in making each item, and how much you can afford to spend on material. Is there a way to save money on materials? Could you use a blend of cheap and expensive material? That should keep down your unit costs and allow a profit margin at the price you have chosen. Now you can make a production plan.

This is a better process for working from market considerations, knowing the competitors and knowing your company's capabilities to finding a price. Buried in that nasty little word "budget" is all the stuff of which overhead dreams are made. Included in them is the business owner's salary.

Let us consider the maxim "pay yourself first." With reference to one's own financial circumstances, this means saving first and then trimming your spending off the balance to make it all fit. In a business, this refers to the owner taking into account any cost and pricing structure, the requirement that he or she gets a paycheck. After all, if the business generates a profit but no salary for the owner, the business is not profitable.

How can we use this piece of intelligence? In the chart below the owner's pay (listed under officers' compensation) is 8 percent of sales. If the owner requires $75,000 a year, then the sales each year must be $937,500. If 8 percent of sales equals $75,000 then what is 100 percent?

TABLE 33
WORKING BACKWARDS

Net Sales	$937,500	100 percent
DIRECT COSTS		
Cost of Goods Sold	$170,000	18 percent
Direct Labor	$430,000	46 percent
Direct of Subcontractor	$ 20,000	2 percent
Other Direct Expenses	$ 67,000	7 percent
Total direct expenses	$687,000	73 percent
GROSS PROFIT	$250,500	27 percent
SALES AND G&A EXPENSES		
Advertising and Promotion	$ 30,000	3 percent
Depreciation	$ 6,890	1 percent
Facilities Expenses	$ 28,000	3 percent
Interest Expenses	$ 1,250	0 percent
Officers' Compensation	$ 75,000	8 percent
Salaries and Commissions	$ 34,000	4 percent
Other Salaries/Commissions	$ 20,000	2 percent
Other Sales Expenses	$ 4,589	0 percent
Other G&A Expenses	$ 5,000	1 percent
TOTAL SALES G&A Expenses	$204,729	22 percent
Net Operating Profit	$ 45,771	5 percent

Don't know where to begin? Earlier in this book I referred to Cost of Doing Business Surveys because they provide just this sort of information. Knowing the percentage of sales for each line item helps you to decide not only if your business is "average" but also to work backwards as in my example here.

Summary

In this chapter, we outlined the broad strokes of financial analysis as they apply to pricing. The math tools examined provide the foundation for a firm understanding of costs so that a business can have realistic pricing. The most important tool is predetermined profitability or the concept of working backwards from costs to the sales figure, rather than trying to make costs fit the sales forecast.

10
DIAGNOSIS AND PRESCRIPTION: WHAT SHOULD I DO TO FIX MY PRICING?

In this chapter we move from detached speculation to a practical application of theory. Not that we can entirely escape theory; all good business decisions begin with a hard look at the facts to see if there really is a pricing problem.

Is there really a pricing problem? Is the problem with pricing or low sales? How do you know?

It has been a long-standing observation of mine through years of small-business consulting work that until a business reaches $30,000 a month in sales, it will have problems paying its bills. 80 percent of the time this is true. This means that price levels are unlikely to be the root cause of the business's profit issue. It simply is not selling enough. But let us suppose that your current sales are adequate but profits are still not there. Here a couple of analyses that may help.

TABLE 34
PRICE INCREASE OR SALES INCREASE?

		With a 9 percent Price Increase	With a 9 percent Increase in Sales Volume
Sales	$300,000	$327,000	$327,000
Cost of Goods Sold (45 percent)	$135,000	$135,000	$147,150
General and Administrative Costs	$ 65,000	$ 65,000	$ 65,000
Profit	$100,000	$127,000	$114,850

Compare a price increase against a sales increase. Would increasing sales by five percent change your bottom line by enough to generate the desired profit? When you have done this calculation, run a similar comparison for a five percent change in prices. Will that change the bottom line enough?

It is tempting to create several "what-if" pictures with sales figures perhaps even double current values. The danger is that the overall financial picture will look really rosy at double the sales volume in most instances. Put away those rose-tinted glasses, unless you have the purchase orders from customers to justify doubling your sales that fast.

Examine your costs. Can you drive them down? Perhaps your pricing is driven by the high cost of your rent or some other large factor in your profit and loss statement.

Are you paying too much for rent, leases, and employees? You will have to do comparison homework here to find out. Getting an industry cost of doing business survey will help you establish how close to the median you are.

If you are a normal business with costs more or less in line, then you probably have a pricing problem. Does the low profit problem arise from the variable or the fixed costs? If the rent is too high or you are supporting too much debt, then can you solve this by reducing rent or paying off debt? Fixed costs drive all prices across the board since every product or service has to generate enough money to cover rent and utilities. High fixed costs leave no wiggle room and cause problems in the business cycle.

Have you made all your best efforts to buy materials or hire labor at the best prices you can? Have you got a decent price from the supplier but are paying freight? Is your business being hammered with a high rate for credit card transactions? Did you buy 85 months' worth of five-part, prenumbered, carbonless, tractor-driven invoices in order to get the price down?

Have you got an ongoing plan to reduce all waste and costs?

If big-box stores can do it, so can you. This should not be solely the job of the owner. Ideally, all staff members participate, looking for ways to cut costs, to do it faster and smarter and not produce so much waste. In fact this is one of the touchstones of lean manufacturing. Lean manufacturing assumes that the people with the screwdrivers on the assembly line know best what causes the delays, what creates the quality issues, and how to make the job simpler.

Where Are You Not Paying Attention?

Typically in any business, there are hundreds of day-to-day items that a business owner has to monitor. And if this year you have paid attention to advertising and its costs, then accounts receivable or another part of your business may have been ignored, to potentially catastrophic consequences.

How can you find this out and assign a dollar value to it? Gather up three or four years' worth of financial statements and convert each line item to a percentage. Put these items into a table like Table 35 and compare year-on-year percentages. They will show you the areas requiring your attention to keep costs under control.

In Table 35, the cost of materials has swung from a low of 17 percent to a high of 28 percent and then, in stages, back to 19 percent. This may be due to the departure of the experienced buyer at the end of year one and his replacement by an inexperienced buyer. In years two, three, and four, the cost of materials falls which indicates the second buyer has gained some control over his or her job. Nevertheless, the second buyer has not gotten costs down to the historical lowest levels. On sales of $575,000 over the four years, the purchaser spent $123,000. If the purchaser had done as great a job as in year one and kept costs to 17 percent, then the purchaser would have spent $97,750 over the same period or a difference of $25,500. Prices should perhaps reflect that higher materials cost.

TABLE 35
HISTORICAL INCOME AND COST ANALYSIS

	Jan 1		Apr 1		Jul 1		Oct 1	
Period Start	Jan 1		Apr 1		Jul 1		Oct 1	
Period End	Mar 31		June 30		Sept 30		Dec 31	
		Percentage of Sales		Percentage of Sales		Percentage of Sales		Percentage of Sales
Gross Sales (Revenue)	$100,000	100	$125,000	100	$150,000	100	$200,000	100
Material	$ 17,000	17	$ 35,000	28	$ 33,000	22	$ 38,000	19
Direct Labor	$ 23,000	23	$ 31,250	25	$ 43,500	29	$ 70,000	35
Subcontractor								
Other								
Cost of Goods Sold								
Net Sales								
Gross Profit								
Sales and G&A Expenses								
Advertising and Promotion	$ 5,000	5	$ 8,750	7	$ 13,500	9	$ 26,000	13
Depreciation								
Facilities								
Interest								
Officers' Compensation								
Salary and Commission								
Other Sales Expenses								
Other G&A Expenses								
Total Sales and G&A Expenses								
Net Operating Profit								

In the direct labor column, the cost of labor has veered sharply upwards. This could be due to several reasons. It could be a hot labor market; accidents have driven up insurance rates, the benefits package costs are higher with an aging workforce — but prices should be anticipating this upward swing.

In the row for advertising, marketing costs have puttered along for three years and suddenly swung upwards in year four. Profits have been non-existent and this upswing is most likely an effort to increase sales.

In this company, if the costs as discussed can not be brought down, then prices must go up or the company will not survive.

What Are You Giving Away for Free That is Not Reflected in Your Prices?

In your profit and loss financial statements, look for freight-in costs, freight-out costs, handling charges, and other items that you pay for and do not pass along to your customers.

In reverse, are you offering free freight and absorbing that cost? Or, have you now got huge receivables because your customers take 60 days to pay and treat you as cheap banking alternative?

How can you find out? Again, from your financial statements, assemble the data. Calculate totals on the freight and other variable and fixed costs. Do your prices cover these items or people? Do you have six people in the back room whose only job is to "jolly along" your customers because you are always late with deliveries?

Now have a look at your balance sheet. Are you a bank and you didn't know it? Have your receivables grown? Did a supplier persuade you to buy a year's worth of inventory all at once to save freight expenses that, of course, he or she would be happy to swallow for such a large order?

In Table 36, the receivables have skyrocketed. If the old levels could be regained, there would be ($34,000 – $5,678) $28,322 more in the bank which would take it from a negative of ($15,000) — presumably a maxed-out overdraft — to $13,322 in the black; Out of the overdraft and not paying interest. Without the interest drawing on cash reserves and with the cash to hunt down specials pricing, costs can be forced to drop.

And what about the inventory? It has also grown and if as a percentage of sales it has leapt up in value over the past four years, then there is a problem. The costs of borrowing the money are not severe like they were in the early 1980s, but the cost of moving "junk" around to find the stuff you need appears in your labor costs and drives your prices or hammers your profits. And, how much of that dead inventory could be recycled for cash, sent back to the supplier for a credit, or simply sold off at cost with a sale? Either way, you need to turn this extra and unneeded inventory into cash.

TABLE 36
HISTORICAL BALANCE SHEET

HISTORICAL BALANCE SHEET				
	ASSETS			
Current Assets	20___	20___	20___	20___
Cash	50,000	23,000	4,678	-15,000
Accounts receivable -trade	5,678	11,000	15,000	34,000
Accounts receivable -notes				
Accounts receivable -other				
Raw materials inventory	27,000	34,000	39,000	55,000
WIP inventory				
Finished goods inventory				
Prepaid expenses				
Short term securities				
Other current assets				
Total Current Assets	$ -	$ -	$ -	$ -
Long Term Assets				
Property				
Plant				
Equipment				
Other fixed assets				
Total fixed assets	$ -	$ -	$ -	$ -
Accumulated depreciation				
Net fixed assets				
Investments				
Investments				
Long term securities				
Other assets				
Total Long Term Assets				
Total ASSETS				
Current Liabilities				
Accounts Payable -Trade				
Accounts Payable - Notes				
Accounts Payable=other				
Accrued payroll expenses				
Accrued payroll taxes				
Accrued PST payable				
Accrued GST payable				
Other accrued expenses				
Total Current Liabilities	$ -	$ -	$ -	$ -
Long Term Debt & Equity				
Long Term Debt & Equity				
Bonds outstanding				
other long term liabilities				
Total long Term Liabilities	$ -	$ -	$ -	$ -
Stock				
Retained Earnings				
Total Liabilities and Equity				

If you can disentangle these costs, can you charge for them separately? Is the warranty separable and therefore a possible up-sell on the original price of the gear? If the manufacturer has a warranty, can you offer any extended warranty that can be sold along with the item? If you are storing prepaid orders awaiting delivery dates and phone calls, are you giving away that premium service? And has it added to your delivery costs?

In this day and age, not many companies can enforce a percentage charge on their account statements. You have to be a monopoly or huge like Visa to do that. So, how can you find ways to make people pay on time or even early, without giving away the shop? Could you afford to give up two percent of volume in order to have invoices paid within ten days?

Examine Your Customer Base. Do You Know What Your Customer Wants?

Can you, in 25 words or less, explain what your typical and best kind of customer looks like? What income, where they live, why they buy from your company?

How do your customers perceive your company? Are you one of many or does your Unique Selling Proposition make you stand out from the crowd? Can you turn this "standing out from the crowd" into cash?

What Need Are You Satisfying for Which You Are Not Charging?

Reread the section on customer stress relief in Chapter 5. If your company has not identified the customer need to solve a problem — whether it is a quality concerns, late delivery concerns, or local repair parts shortage concerns — then you do not have a good Unique Selling Proposition. You really don't know what your customer wants.

Check your Unique Selling Proposition

As discussed in Chapter 4, a good Unique Selling Proposition (USP) has the following characteristics:

- Your USP highlights a specific benefit to be had from using the company or buying the product.

- The proposition itself must be unique — something that competitors do not, or will not, offer.

- The proposition must be strong enough to pull new customers to the product.

- It is short.

- It paints a mental picture.

- The differences highlighted must be substantial.

When you have a USP, make sure that it is incorporated in all your communications to potential customers. Also ensure that it is well understood by your whole team and consistently delivered on. You will attract a strong following of loyal customers and your business will thrive.

Test the Waters

You can instruct your sales staff to test the waters gently by talking about price before one is quoted. That way you might just get lucky and the customer will tell you what price they want to pay.

Train Your Staff

Retraining your staff to sell features, advantages and benefits (FAB) rather than price can be a real challenge but it is worthwhile. Start with something important but small. For example, a feature would be heavy-duty springs, the advantage is that they support a heavier load easily and the benefit the customer is buying is that they get more work done without the risk of breaking the springs. Work towards the larger ones and very soon into the process, teach them your company's Unique Selling Proposition so that it gets sold along with the product, adding value because you are explaining the uniqueness of your company's products and services to the customer.

Finally, train your salespeople to make Request For Quote (RFQ) presentations. It is not all about price. Emphasize the benefits of buying from your company before you get to the bottom line. Make certain you are talking to the person with the authority to sign the purchase order. More than one deal has unraveled because the time spent on building a relationship with the buyer collapsed when the boss said no just because of the price. Remember to sandwich your price between benefits. *"This roof will last 30 years and has a leak-free warranty from the manufacturer for 12 years. The full price can be paid in 3 installments of $2,000 totaling $6,000 plus taxes and we can start 13 days ahead of the competition."*

Test Different Pricing Strategies

You need not limit yourself to just a bald price sitting on the desk for everyone to see.

- Consider framing your price so that your product will gain the customer a benefit or prevent a loss.

- Consider beginning your price negotiation with the most feature-filled, expensive product you have on the shelf. Then take features away as the price drops.

- Consider reference pricing. Bottled water sells for more per liter than gasoline.

- Consider framing your prices in proportional price evaluation layers with the competition. For example, "My barbecue burner is $1.50 more than the local large chain store's, but mine is OEM and theirs only requires some Saturday afternoon assembly to get it to work."

- Consider introducing price changes in segmented product lines or services or to easily-identified segments of your customer list as opposed to a large price increase on every item.

- Consider a strategy of penetration pricing to gain sudden and overwhelming market share.

- Consider market skimming and introduce your new product at the top end of the market for early adopters, and then slowly slide the price downwards to gather succeeding layers of the market.

Going from Analysis to Action:
Implementing a Price Increase

You have done all the analytical work and found that your prices are low and are the cause of lost profitability. All avenues to reduce costs have been put under the microscope and explored twice over but will not lead to enough of an increase in profits.

What to do now? Obviously there is a call to action if all this high level analytical work is not to be wasted. Do you then just raise prices? What about the reaction of existing customers? What about your reputation in the industry? What about existing contract prices? Will your competition follow suit and raise prices or will they attack like a pack of ravenous wolves?

Most business owners would have nightmares about massive price hikes and the consequences of having existing customers leave them for the competition.

In an example related by Justin Martin for Fortune Small Business,[48] the CEO is confronted by this exact dilemma. The company made eight types of dry film lubricants and protective coatings. The client base included NASCAR drivers, professional drag racers, and monster-truckers, who use the product to keep their engines running smoothly. The owner was meeting their expenses each month but they just kept rising: bills for materials, salaries for his employees, insurance and premiums.

For the past three years, prices had not moved. The owner was winning new customers, but with his prices fixed and costs climbing, he was seeing his profit margin shrink at a rate of five percentage points a year. Could he raise prices. He was afraid of losing customers if he initiated a dramatic price rise.

Losses loomed on the horizon, so the CEO took a deep breath and announced price hikes that averaged 18 percent. The company's customers stayed put, and they saw an instant boost to the bottom line. The CEO expects the firm to raise $3 million in revenues in 2007, up from $2.6 million in 2006, and to pocket healthy profits as well. "I was surprised by how much leeway we have on what we charge," said the CEO.

---

48. *Raising prices, keeping customers.* Justin Martin, *Fortune Small Business*, September 13 2007

So some customers will leave you. But it is not all bad. Consider the upside of increasing prices. Some customers will leave. They are the customers who are not loyal and buy only on price. It does not matter whether you are the only auto-body shop in town that supplies a Ferrari as a loaner car, this type of customer does not care. So all the extra costs that you shoulder to offer a truly terrific service are a waste of money on that customer. Do you really need him or her? Is this a Mrs. Crabapple, driving up your costs?

Having concluded that the company's salvation lies only in increasing prices here are several implementation strategies:

- Jack up your prices. David Jenkins of Kelowna explained how it worked in his business: "I went through this years ago selling resin to the BC plywood industry. For years we had given them pricing based on raw material costs plus a small profit. Yes, it protected us from losing money but it in no way allowed us upward flexibility. It took a very hard stance on our part and a willingness to walk away from the business to get this changed."

- Go slowly — a steady trickle of price increases is likely better received than a single torrent of increases. Increasing all your prices across the board by some massive number will probably work against your company. Better to have a series of small increases unevenly distributed across the spectrum of your products and services. A single big increase becomes the talk of the industry — "Did you hear that Anderson's just jacked up prices 45 percent yesterday?" A big increase will alert your competition and they could use it against you.

- But let us consider this problem from the point of view of a distributor, a multi-faceted service business, or a retail business. In these companies, the customers only really know the prices of 10 or so items. Given sensitivity to a limited range of prices, there is scope with powerful enough software to price belts or oil changes differently for one customer than another. So the solution would be to listen to these customers and identify these 10 or 50 items. With the right software you can begin the process of de-constructing your price list.

- Warning: If your business is about to close its doors due to financial problems arising from low prices, you do not have the time to play games. The consequences of doing further testing and analyzing are that your business will fold. And if you immediately implement a truly shocking price increase, some customers will leave, but the business will not fold today. Raise prices now.

- A strategy of telling customers that prices are under review will be less shocking than a wholesale unannounced across-the-board increase. Customers will only care about or be sensitive to products and service increases that effect their business.

- Can you unbundle your product or service? If you have an item that normally sells for $45 as a kit, can you successfully take that kit apart and sell the components for higher prices and more profit? Could you, like a software vendor who offers full, service packages, offer to the price sensitive customers a "no increase" package that strips way the services they do not use anyway but which add to your costs?

- Similarly, can you bundle a single item or service with some add-on and charge more than the mere sum of its pieces? Your package would then change from a simple oil change to a 70-point check of the car's fluids and electrical system. If you are a service company, offering a small up-sell service can increase the dollar value of your overall product and decrease costs by reducing travel time. Or if you are a bakery with an average $5 invoice per customer, adding a $2 cookie to each sale by positioning impulse cookies for sale by the cash register lowers your cost per transaction and is almost as effective as increasing prices.

- Or consider this problem from the point of view of a company that does one thing or sells one product line, like a car dealer. There are core prices — (as advertised on TV!) — leaving little wriggle room to hike up prices. So the change has to be in the add-on services or products that are a key part of the Unique Selling Proposition. If you are a plumber called out to a leaky faucet for example, the add-on would be an inspection of the overall under-sink plumbing and installing a replacement or new carburetor. This does not necessarily raise prices but it does increase profit since the fixed costs of getting a man into the house are already paid, leaving every extra profit dollar in your pocket.

- Do you have to increase prices to all customers? Consider that you have long-time customers who buy 40 cases of your worm killer product each month and have done so, religiously, every year for a decade. Do your new customers who have been just now persuaded to use your worm killer, deserve the same level of pricing? Probably not, but how do you explain this to a new customer? If they are willing to issue a purchase order committing to the purchase of 40 cases of worm killer product per month over the next 10 years and pay on the 30th day, then perhaps they are deserving of the same pricing structure.

Years ago, I spoke with a fellow business analyst who explained that a company he had recently visited sold custom tanks each year to three customers. Two of the customers generated all the profit and the third customer — a huge multi-national conglomerate — lost them all of the profit and more. The answer was obvious to me; they needed to stop selling to this huge customer or find a different pricing structure. But the client could not get past the idea of raising prices to profitable levels because the thought of volunteering to let one third of his business go was too much.

Summary

Fix your pricing today by asking the all important questions and taking action.

This chapter was designed to draw your attention to areas that are often ignored in the day-to-day running of a business. Attack your costs with vigor if you can realistically compress them enough to make a difference in your bottom line. If not, then increase prices today.

Take a hard look at what you offer along with your product or service. These are things that have been built up over the years — extra checks, extra service. Do you really need them? what are you giving away free with your product that is not reflected in your prices?

Again, develop a truly startling Unique Selling Proposition. Without this statement of what makes your company different, this statement woven into the very fabric of your universe and the universe of your employees, it will be difficult to justify price increases. After you have the USP, train your staff to use it and how to respond to price objections from customers.

And finally, go from analysis to action and implement a price increase.

11
TRUE LIFE BUSINESS SCENARIOS: THE CASE STUDIES

Paying Attention to Pricing: Examples from Other Companies

In a 2002 article[49], *The Economist* magazine examined the importance of finding the correct price. Several clever companies had found ways to boost prices but too many were still getting it wrong.

Raising prices is likely to remain hard work even as the world economy chugs along to new heights. Inflation is likely to remain low in rich countries. Globalization has vastly increased the number of competitors. The Internet has made it easier for buyers to shop around and to compare prices. Big buyers, such as Wal-Mart, are squeezing ever more from their suppliers. The days of annual and upward changes to price lists look to be finished.

Who has struggled with keeping prices right for their business and industry?

In a 2002 MIT Sloan Management Review article entitled "Pricing as a Strategic Capability," authors Bergen, Levy, Ritson, Zbaracki and Dutta cite Polaroid, which went bust in 2001 largely because it failed to price its digital-photography products properly.

---

49. "The price is wrong." *The Economist,* May 23rd 2002

Who has succeeded in pricing their goods and services correctly and how did they do it?

Understanding their pricing policies and customers has helped airlines for decades. Consider the impact of the Internet on buying airline tickets. The internet should have flattened prices. Instead, there is a price differential by perhaps as much as double for a ticket purchased in Canada versus the same ticket bought in the United States. The airlines keep the prices separate by not accepting Canadian credit cards on line.

The airlines have, for decades, played with their sophisticated yield-management systems to maximize profits. They identify and address whole categories of customers based on willingness to pay. Now, other companies from retailers to chemical plants have slowly started to follow due to downward pressure on prices.

Whirlpool, an American appliance maker, says it overhauled its pricing by thinking of prices themselves as a product, much like a dishwasher. Despite a fall in demand, when steep price cuts were the traditional response to keep the assembly lines humming and market share intact, Whirlpool reduced the frequency of its discounts, which it said were costly to communicate to salespeople, and confused customers if they were changed too often.

Then it was noted that the American subsidiary of Roche, a Swiss drug company, allowed complete latitude to its sales force and that each price was set on the merits of each deal. One of its top managers, Ron Andrews, introduced software for every salesperson's laptop computer to provide instant and profitable price quotes in the field. But this was not enough to change a corporate culture that saw pricing as a tactical measure to get each deal rather than pricing as a strategic option to increase sales, market share, and company position. To help, he created a new post for a Director of Pricing Strategy.

A popular and unfortunately crude pricing method is often employed by car dealerships. In this technique of hidden or "stealth" increases, there are extra charges for features such as anti-lock brakes and passenger-side airbags, instead of offering them as standard features. So the dealership advertises an absurdly low price and the potential buyer is given only a platform, small engine and a steering wheel. "You want tires with that, too? That will be extra."

A somewhat more subtle approach is to offer a huge menu of financing schemes. By giving the customer plenty of choices he or she will struggle to find the deal with the cheapest price.

Industrial markets are even more demanding. Dow Chemical, operating in the dull but brutal commodity-plastics market, identified add-on services that it once provided in an all-in-one price for its products. These are now priced separately. For a range of fees, Dow has begun offering faster delivery, pay-per-use technical support, and consultants to help customers use their plastics more efficiently.

Today's managers have a vast array of sophisticated fancy technology to help them. Supermarket chains, for example, can quickly and easily track customers' "elasticity;" how their buying habits change in response to a price increase or a discount.

Case Study
Pocket Price Banding — Castle Battery

The Castle Battery Company Case shows how one company used the pocket price waterfall and band to identify profit leaks and regain control of its pricing system. It illustrates one way in which the waterfall and band concepts can be applied, and shows how, if a company doesn't manage its pricing policies on all levels, experienced customers may be working those policies to their own advantage.

The Castle Battery Company is a manufacturer of replacement lead-acid batteries for automobiles. Castle's direct customers are auto-parts distributors, auto-parts retailers, and some general mass merchandisers. With return on sales averaging in the 7 percent range, Castle's profitability is very sensitive to even small improvements in price: A 1 percent increase in price with no volume loss, for instance, would increase operating profit dollars by 14 percent.

Extreme overcapacity in the battery industry and gradual commoditization made it increasingly difficult for Castle to distinguish its products from competitors. So Castle senior management was skeptical that there was much, if any, potential for price improvement. But Castle managers had entirely overlooked lucrative pricing opportunities at the transaction level.

Table 37 shows the typical pocket price waterfall for one of Castle's common battery models, the Power-Lite, sold to an auto parts retailer. From a base price of $28.40, Castle deducted standard dealer/distributor and order-size discounts. The company also subtracted an on-invoice exception discount, negotiated on a customer-by-customer basis to "meet competition." With these discounts, the invoice price to the retailer totaled $21.16. What little transaction price monitoring that Castle did focused exclusively on invoice.

That focus ignored a big part of the pricing picture — off-invoice discounting. Castle allowed cash discounts of 1.2 percent for timely payments by accounts. Additionally, the company granted extended terms (payment not required until 60 or 90 days after receipt of a shipment) as part of promotional programs or on an exception basis. For this transaction, the extra cost of carrying these extended receivables totaled 22 cents. Cooperative advertising, where Castle contributed to its accounts' local advertising of Castle products, cost 85 cents. A special merchandising program in effect at the time of this transaction discounted another 60 cents. An annual volume rebate, based on total volume and paid at year-end, decreased revenues by yet another 74 cents, and freight paid by Castle for shipping the battery to the retailer cost 32 cents.

TABLE 37
OFF-INVOICE DISCOUNTS: A BIG PART OF THE PRICING STRUCTURE

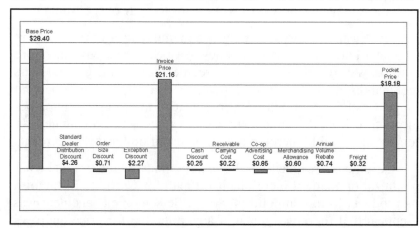

The invoice price minus this long list of off-invoice items resulted in a pocket price of only $18.18, a full 14 percent less than on the invoice. The total revenue drop from base price down to pocket price is the "pocket discount" — in this case, $10.22, of which $2.98 was off-invoice.

Of course, not all transactions for this particular model of battery had the same pocket price. As Table 38 shows, each element of the pocket price waterfall varied widely by customer and transaction, resulting in a very broad pocket price band. While the average pocket price was $20, units sold for as high as $25 and as low as $14 — plus or minus greater than 25 percent around the average. A price band like this should trigger immediate questions: What are the underlying drivers of the band's shape and width? Why are pocket prices so variable, and can that variability be positively managed?

TABLE 38
A SINGLE PRODUCT CAN HAVE A WIDE POCKET PRICE BAND

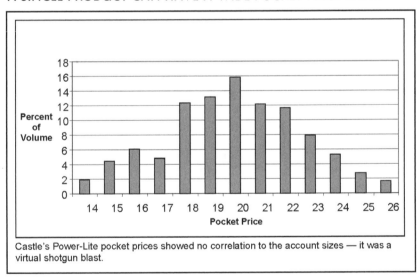

Castle's Power-Lite pocket prices showed no correlation to the account sizes — it was a virtual shotgun blast.

Castle managers were quite surprised at the width of the price band for their Power-Lite model, but on reflection, concluded that it was due to differences in account sizes. The company had a clear strategy of rewarding account volume with lower price, rationalizing that cost to serve would decrease with account volume.

But when management examined the Power-Lite pocket prices against total account sizes for a sample of 50 accounts, it found no correlation — it was a virtual shotgun blast. A number of relatively small accounts were buying at very low pocket prices while some very large accounts were buying at very high pocket price levels.

Castle managers, perplexed by the scatter of pocket prices by account size, launched an immediate investigation. In most cases, they found no legitimate reason why certain low-volume accounts were paying such discounted prices. Often, they discovered that these accounts were unusually experienced and clever accounts-customers who had been dealing with Castle for 20 years or more and who knew just whom to call at Castle headquarters to get that extra exception discount, that percentage point of additional co-op advertising, that extra 30 or 60 days to pay. These favorite old accounts were granted extra discounts based on familiarity and relationships rather than on economic justification. These experienced clients understood Castle's pocket price waterfall and were working it against the company.

Castle senior management realized that its transaction pricing process was out of control, that decision making up and down the waterfall lacked discipline, and that no one was focusing on the comprehensive total of those decisions. The end result was a pricing reality that didn't square with Castle's strategy of rewarding account size with lower prices, and that was costing Castle millions.

To correct its transaction pricing situation, Castle mounted a three-part program. First, it took very aggressive corrective actions to bring the overdiscounted, "old favorite" accounts back in line. Management identified the problem accounts and explained the situation and its impact on overall company profits to the sales force. Then the company gave the sales force nine months to fix or drop those outliers. Fixing meant decreasing the excessive discounting across the waterfall so that outlier accounts' pocket prices were more in line with those of accounts of similar size. Salespeople who couldn't negotiate their outlier pocket prices up to an appropriate level were to find other accounts in their territory to replace them.

Within the time allotted, the sales force fixed 90 percent of the trouble accounts. Sales' newfound realization that every element of the waterfall represented a viable negotiating lever contributed to this success. And, in most cases, the salespeople easily found profitable replacements for the other 10 percent.

Second, Castle launched a program to stimulate volume in larger accounts that had higher than average pocket prices compared with accounts of similar size. Management singled out the attractive "target" accounts for special treatment. Sales and marketing personnel investigated them carefully to determine the nonprice benefits to which each was most sensitive. The company increased volume in these accounts not by lowering price but by delivering the specific benefits that were most important to each: higher service levels for some, shortened order lead times for others, more frequent sales calls for still others.

Finally, Castle embarked on a crash program to get the transaction pricing process back under control. This program included, among other components, setting clear decision rules for each discretionary item in the waterfall. For example, the company capped exception discounts at 5 percent and granted them only after a specific volume and margin impact evaluation. Management also set up new information systems to guide and monitor transaction pricing decisions. And Castle established pocket price as the universal measure of price performance in all of these systems. It began to track and assign, transaction-by-transaction, all of the significant off-invoice waterfall elements that were previously collected and reported only on a companywide basis. Further, pocket price realization became a major component of the incentive, compensation of salespeople sales managers and product managers.

Castle reaped rich and sustained rewards from these three transaction pricing initiatives. In the first year, average pocket price levels increased 3 percent and, even though volume remained flat operating profits swelled 42 percent. The company realized additional pocket price gains in each of the two subsequent years.

Castle also received some unexpected strategic benefits from its newfound transaction pricing capability. Account-specific pocket price reporting revealed a small but growing distribution channel where Castle pocket prices were consistently higher than average. Increasing volume and penetration in this emerging channel became one of Castle's key strategic initiatives this past year. The fresh and more detailed business perspective that Castle senior managers gained from their transaction pricing involvement became the catalyst for an ongoing stream of similar strategic insights. [50]

---

50. *HARVARD BUSINESS REVIEW* "Managing Price, Gaining Profit" September - October 1992

Case Study
GENERIC Truck and Diesel Ltd. "Resetting the Clock"

March 11, 2005

Overview

In essence, GENERIC Truck and Diesel is a business worth salvaging for its ability to generate a retirement nest egg for the owners. Its past 10 years of poor financial performance can easily be turned around and it can again be made into a profitable business — even in the current economic climate. And if the economy revives in the Main City to Smallville corridor, local companies overall will be busy again.

I have not answered anywhere in this report why the company got into trouble. That is not important. The company's history just shows us what not to repeat. Nevertheless, the staff are certain of whom to blame and the loss of trust in the current management and ownership is serious. To remedy that, some of my recommendations are personnel based. In brief, this company can no longer be a family concern in order to operate and be sold profitably. The company needs to embrace the best methods employed by modern companies to cut out the non-performing bits and forge ahead armed with a plan.

This plan falls into two parts:

1. Bandages: What needs to be done immediately with regards to reforming the parts department, the service department, personnel and getting basic business information in front of the owner.

2. Treatment: The longer term business systems projects that enhance profits and codify procedures and methods. Codifying means that any outsider can buy and run the business with minimum training, thereby enhancing the business selling price.

Parts Department

Analysis

1. The parts department is untidy and dirty enough to make it a difficult place to work and truly discouraging for the staff. I had expected that with the low volumes that the shelves would be organised and tidy.

2. There is $45,000 worth of dead stock from Supplier Z alone. The dead stock is the result of inattention by the parts department and means that $45,000 of cash was taken from GENERIC Truck's bottom line with no return on that investment. With 40 percent margins before the parts labor is added, the dead stock value translates into countless lost dollars in over the counter sales and repair jobs. This amount of dead stock has grown to this level from zero after the building burned.

3. Although the parts manager was diligent on the single purchase order I saw completed, the other staff and Miss A. have informed that this is not usually the case. While the current COD basis for buying parts is in place, poor paperwork procedures have no impact other than creating unnecessary confusion in the parts department (no names and prices). Soon this paperwork will be needed for cash flow projections.

4. The backorder system in Rinax (ERP computer system) is not used leading to confusion over what is ordered for whom, when it will be in and creating a dependence upon someone's memory.

5. Parts leave the building without being charged. Given the dire financial straits in which the company finds itself, this is outrageous and totally unnecessary.

6. Anecdotally, I was told that customers occasionally leave the building with parts charged on their accounts when they should have been paying cash. Rinax must be able to link together the accounts receivable and invoicing systems to stop this from happening.

7. There was a $20,000 variance in the inventory at last count. This information came from the Parts Manager and I did

not verify this. This number is too high and is a further indicator of sloppy controls. A variance of 1—5 percent is appropriate in a parts department.

8. The parts department does not up-sell to customers. It has no notion of its breakeven sales volume, so it operates in a vacuum. The breakeven according to the October 31 figures is $19,567 per week including sales to the service department.

9. The conflicts that exist between the parts department and the service department are destructive if understandable in the company's current situation. Service blames the parts for poor performance and has only a dim understanding of the cash constraints. Most importantly the service department believes the parts staff think of them as an annoyance as opposed to a partner in the business.

10. The staff complain that the parts manager is absent when needed, indeed absent too much.

Solutions

1. Clean up the parts shelves.

2. Tighter inventory controls. Items that will become dead stock will always be purchased. That is part of being in the parts business. But Supplier Z and other vendors will take back inventory under certain terms and conditions and time frames. The parts department needs to be vigilant about this number — the dollar value of inventory over 270 days — and present this figure to the owner monthly on his wall white board. Together with the number of days old that the inventory is, and the dollar value of cores and warranty parts not yet returned, this will give the owner all the information he needs to see that the parts department is controlling the cash outlay.

3. When the elbow room is created to buy parts inventory again, only the fastest moving "A" parts should be purchased for the first 6 months. This will guarantee that the room created by the returns and new financial picture are maximized. Purchases of items NOT on the "A" list should be treated as special order and a 70 percent deposit collected to cover the cost of the parts (60 percent of the sale value) and freight. Moreover, when the part arrives, it should be

immediately invoiced to the customer and the bill sent out. This will improve cash flow.

4. In the longer term, the parts department needs to use the Rinax backorder system to control parts ordered for customers. The backorder system is needed to create credibility with customers and its immediate activation will be simpler now than when the department gets really busy again. When the system is underway, the backorder report needs to be printed weekly and reviewed by the owner and the parts manager. The total length of the report is the first indicator to the owner about whether the parts department is doing its job. The second indicator is the age of the backorders.

5. Purchase orders filled out completely need to go to accounting as input into the cash flow figures. Purchases of $20,000 this week on purchase orders means that in some 30 days the company must be able to write a cheque for $20,000 and the finance department needs to know this in advance.

6. When the purchase orders start becoming useful input to the cash flow figures, the finance department's weekly cash flow meetings can produce a weekly budget figure for the parts department. Armed with a budget, the parts manager can afford to buy non-essentials for the add-on sales.

7. Uncharged parts. The service and parts department can work together better to control parts leaving the building. Currently the service manager chases down what he hopes was used on the work orders because nothing is written down on the work order. I suggest strongly that the mechanic take the work order from the gray table to the parts counter so that the parts man can write the part on the work order while it is fresh in his mind. No work order, no parts.

8. A paperwork flow chart will unearth the areas where the systems have holes, where unnecessary steps are taken and where unnecessary paper is kept.

9. Variance in inventory can be brought under control by counting the inventory more often, I suggest that the entire inventory be verified as soon as is possible and that, bi-weekly, some part of the inventory is counted to verify the

numbers. The dollar value is important but more importantly, and peculiar to parts businesses, having nine pieces of ten cent "c" clips on the shelf instead of the ten your mechanic or customer needs to finish a job is critical. Counting some portion of the inventory at regular intervals becomes habit forming after awhile, fills the slow periods, increases confidence in the validity of the numbers you see on screen, and makes all stock taking easier. The owner needs to see that all the divisions of the inventory are counted regularly by a report from the parts manager showing the variance and what date each section was counted.

10. Pricing issues. If the service department charges parts at a 15 percent premium on average, this will add $ 102,198 dollars to the bottom line generating a profit of 5.5 percent. The owner needs to keep this number in front of the service manager's face at all items to make certain that it happens.

11. Wal-Mart pricing, otherwise known as marginal pricing, is a tactic to create extra profits and margins while also creating the impression of being the "cheapest" source in town. Attached is the explanation using lawnmowers as the example. The same tactics can be used to help the owner or the forthcoming sales person to buy back old customers and up sell. The tactic should for the moment, be used only on consumable items where the owner can say to the customer, buy ten cases and get one free without impact on the margins.

12. The owner can help the parts department focus on its job by posting the breakeven dollar volume for the department to see and referring to it often. This figure needs to be reviewed to keep it true and accurate. This focus will also help morale in the service department because the parts department will start seeing the service department as customers and contributors to its weekly targets instead of an annoyance.

13. The company needs a salesman other than the owner. The Owner's skills and presence is needed in the company with attention first to the parts department and then the service department. As parts become available again, the owner can train a salesperson to make the rounds.

In this example, a parts and service company found itself in trouble and, like many companies, let its controls and metrics lapse. My three-day review of the situation, partly reproduced here, focused on rebuilding those controls and finding areas — some small — where money was to be found. Pricing and adding value play a large part in this study.

Best of all, we found that the parts department was in total disarray and was sitting atop $30,000 worth of items that could be exchanged for a substantial credit with its major supplier, thereby creating operating capital.

Summary

The trick is to move prices without annoying customers. Most owners and managers assume they can change prices often and with a minor amount of effort. But this too heavily discounts the costs of management time, as well as risks alienating some customers while appeasing others. Once a bad price is established, it can be devilish to fix.

Does the result reward the effort to make prices better? Although firms can now measure price elasticity in a more sophisticated way, basic rules of thumb are still the most common way of setting price.

And yet most bosses still worry more about their costs than about the prices they charge. A survey found that managers spent less than 10 percent of their time on pricing. But could this time be better spent? Henry Vogel of the Boston Consulting Group likes to remind clients that raising prices by 1 percent can boost profits by up to 4 times as much as a 1 percent cut in overheads and fixed costs.

Chief executives need to pay more attention to pricing. There is a need to go beyond today's narrow view rules of thumb and to invest in pricing capital, better computer models and systems as well as price-savvy managers. But these may be difficult to find, as few business schools teach pricing as a discipline; instead, they see it as a branch of marketing.

APPENDIX I
CALCULATING GROSS MARGIN VERSUS MARKUP

Gross margin is the profit portion of the sale price expressed as a percentage of the sale price.

profit ÷ sale price = profit margin or margin

Markup is the factor by which you multiply the cost to achieve the final sales price.

cost X factor = selling price

These two ways to express price and profit are hugely different as the calculations below reveal but the importance is that banks and accountants use GROSS MARGIN almost exclusively.

Markup versus Gross Margin

	Cost		Yields Selling Price	Profit
Markup 45 percent	$ 125	times 1.45	$ 181.25	$ 56.25
Gross Margin 45 percent	$ 125	divided by .55	$ 227.27	$ 102.27

Where did the "divide by .55" come from?

A margin of 45 percent means necessarily that 55 percent is cost. Simple mathematics shows that 100 percent (the selling price) minus the cost of 55 percent, comes to 45 percent.

Simple algebra shows that to find the selling price you take the cost at $125 and divide by the gross margin percentage (55) to get the selling price in the equation below:

**cost in dollars ÷ gross margin in percent =
selling price in dollars**

And to find your gross margin percentage you divide the profit by the total selling price as in the equation below.

**selling price minus cost ÷ selling price =
gross margin percentage**

APPENDIX II
FIXED AND VARIABLE COSTS

What Is Fixed Cost and Its Impact On My Profits?

Fixed costs include rent, utilities, insurance, vehicle leases, salaries, and taxes, among other possibilities. Their common characteristic is that the business has no choice but to pay them every month whether the doors are open or closed.

Variable Costs include hourly wages, vehicle fuel, materials, advertising, freight, and other possibilities. Their characteristic is that if the doors closed these costs would shrink to nothing or almost nothing.

This is important because a high fixed cost means that the sales target each month is large and sometimes insurmountable. If fixed costs are $8,000 a month and gross margin is 35 percent (profit on sales) then the first $22,857 of sales each month goes to pay the fixed costs. In other words, for each $100 in sales, $35 goes to paying overhead and the balance is used to pay the cost of materials and labour to produce the good or service. Beyond that point, each sale contributes something to the bottom line and the more that is sold the bigger the profit.

$$\$8,000 \div .35 = \$22,857$$

Impact of Fixed Costs on Sales Targets

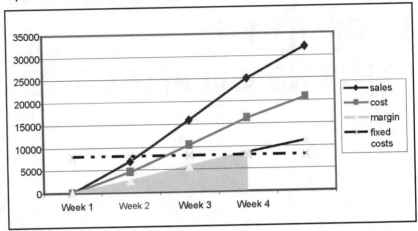

In this chart, the solid color area is the "gross profit" generated by each sale. Variable costs are accounted for and paid as the week progresses in order to focus on the impact of fixed costs. The broken line is the fixed cost which rumbles along each month oblivious to the efforts and troubles of the company. Somewhere, in this example, between week three and the end of the month, the fixed costs are paid for and since the variable costs area being paid all the way along, that magic profit wedge enters the picture.

If, on the other hand, fixed costs are $6,000 a month and the gross margin remains the same at 35 percent, then only the first $17,142.85 of sales is needed to "crack the nut."

$$6,000 \div .35 = 17,142.85$$

Keep fixed costs as low as possible. In a bad month, the business can still pay the bills it must pay. When considering a business expense look at how long you are being tied to that expense. Is it better to take the short term pain of paying cash or the long term monthly payment? This makes the business nimbler and able to respond more quickly to changes in the market place.

And what impact does this have on pricing? Being more flexible makes it simpler to take the hits when necessary.

Consider that a fictional business's situation is that the only projected sale for the month is $50,000. Fixed costs are $18,000 and variable costs are 65 percent. Can you afford to drop the price to make this all important sale?

$50,000   sale

$18,000   fixed cost

$32,500   variable costs

$50,500   total costs

What is variable cost and its impact on my profits?

By definition, variable costs change with how much is produced.

In the printing industry, the cost of setting up the printer is the fixed cost and the variable cost is the paper, and ink, and shop time. So, making 500 business cards may be $25 but making 10,000 business cards will NOT be a simple multiple of $25 totaling $500 but some lower number based upon the variable costs of ink, paper and runtime.

Essentially the fixed costs of the setup time and plant overhead is spread over the entire production run in this standard cost accounting formula.

APPENDIX III
ANALYZING YOUR FINANCIAL STATEMENTS

Bookkeepers everywhere will hate me for suggesting that you ask for financial statements that incorporate the following features:

1. All line items should be expressed as a percentage of gross sales.

   E.g.   Sales $125,000   100 percent

         Cost of goods $ 43,000   34.4 percent

2. Where possible, each line item should have a history to show what the figure was last year at this time or what the figure was for the same period last year.

E.g.	2006	2005
Cost of goods	34.4 percent	37.2 percent

   or

Sales	Aug 2006	Aug 2005
	$10,416.67	$9,876.35

   Ideally, the historical figures should show at least two years. I have found in practice that having four years of history tells a huge story.

3. Where possible, all items above the gross margin line should be your direct costs. Many times I have seen financial statements where the labour cost of a firm that buys and sells labour is treated as administrative cost, so the true cost of doing business is hidden.

E.g.

Before	Sales	$125,000
	Cost of goods	$ 43,000
	Margin	$ 82,000
	Admin	$ 65,000
	Profit	$ 17,000
After	Sales	$125,000
	Cost of goods	$ 43,000
	Cost of labour	$ 65,000
	Margin	$ 17,000

From the $17,000 margin, the owner, rent and utilities can be paid.

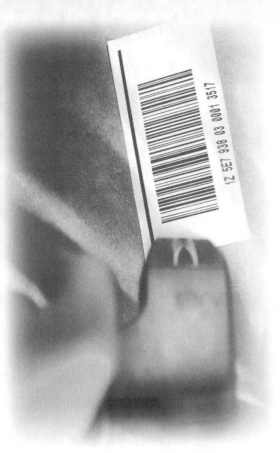

APPENDIX IV
CALCULATING RETURN ON INVESTMENT

Canada is, according to Statistics Canada, an under-investor in capital equipment. The United states, meanwhile, has seen its productivity soar in the past decade or more due to investment in tools — knowledge or otherwise — that magnify the labor component of a company's costs and create a situation whereby more is done with less.

But the measure of success is partly productivity gains and partly the return on this investment in capital goods. Knowing whether to buy an expensive machine to make widgets more quickly is a math exercise. The diagrams that follow have been developed and used for decades by companies such as DuPont and others, and show how to calculate the Return on Investment figure.

The Return on Investment chart shows a technique that can used to analyze the profitability of a company using traditional performance management tools. To enable this, the model integrates elements of the Income Statement with those of the Balance Sheet.

Strength and Benefits of the Return on Investment model

- Simplicity. This is a very basic tool to teach department managers and employees the impact of their actions upon the

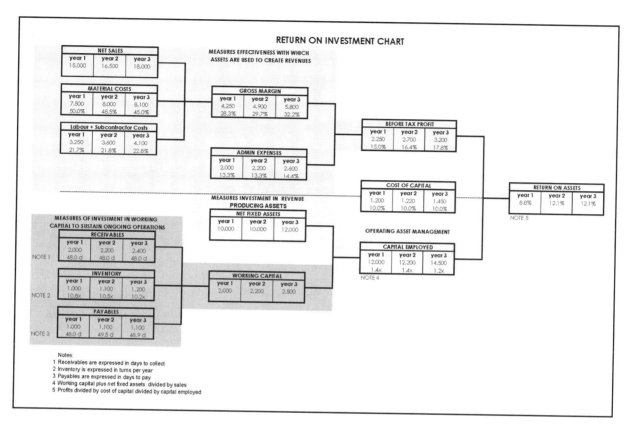

RETURN ON INVESTMENT CHART

MEASURES EFFECTIVENESS WITH WHICH
ASSETS ARE USED TO CREATE REVENUES

NET SALES		
year 1	year 2	year 3
15,000	16,500	18,000

MATERIAL COSTS		
year 1	year 2	year 3
7,500	8,000	8,100
50.0%	48.5%	45.0%

Labour + Subcontractor Costs		
year 1	year 2	year 3
3,250	3,600	4,100
21.7%	21.8%	22.8%

GROSS MARGIN		
year 1	year 2	year 3
4,250	4,900	5,800
28.3%	29.7%	32.2%

ADMIN EXPENSES		
year 1	year 2	year 3
2,000	2,200	2,600
13.3%	13.3%	14.4%

BEFORE TAX PROFIT		
year 1	year 2	year 3
2,250	2,700	3,200
15.0%	16.4%	17.8%

COST OF CAPITAL		
year 1	year 2	year 3
1,200	1,220	1,450
10.0%	10.0%	10.0%

RETURN ON ASSETS		
year 1	year 2	year 3
8.8%	12.1%	12.1%
NOTE 5

MEASURES INVESTMENT IN REVENUE
PRODUCING ASSETS

NET FIXED ASSETS		
year 1	year 2	year 3
10,000	10,000	12,000

MEASURES OF INVESTMENT IN WORKING
CAPITAL TO SUSTAIN ONGOING OPERATIONS

RECEIVABLES		
year 1	year 2	year 3
2,000	2,200	2,400
48.0 d	48.0 d	48.0 d
NOTE 1

INVENTORY		
year 1	year 2	year 3
1,000	1,100	1,200
10.8x	10.5x	10.2x
NOTE 2

PAYABLES		
year 1	year 2	year 3
1,000	1,100	1,100
48.0 d	49.5 d	48.9 d
NOTE 3

WORKING CAPITAL		
year 1	year 2	year 3
2,000	2,200	2,500

OPERATING ASSET MANAGEMENT

CAPITAL EMPLOYED		
year 1	year 2	year 3
12,000	12,200	14,500
1.4x	1.4x	1.2x
NOTE 4

Notes:
1 Receivables are expressed in days to collect
2 Inventory is expressed in turns per year
3 Payables are expressed in days to pay
4 Working capital plus net fixed assets divided by sales
5 Profits divided by cost of capital divided by capital employed

profitability and viability of the company.

• Can easily be linked to compensation schemes.

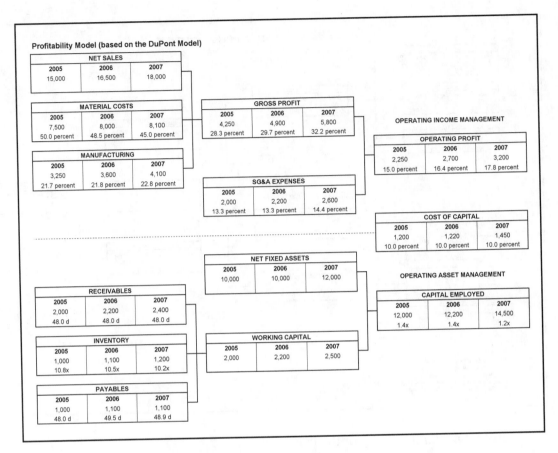

Profitability Model (based on the DuPont Model)

NET SALES

2005	2006	2007
15,000	16,500	18,000

MATERIAL COSTS

2005	2006	2007
7,500	8,000	8,100
50.0 percent	48.5 percent	45.0 percent

MANUFACTURING

2005	2006	2007
3,250	3,600	4,100
21.7 percent	21.8 percent	22.8 percent

GROSS PROFIT

2005	2006	2007
4,250	4,900	5,800
28.3 percent	29.7 percent	32.2 percent

SG&A EXPENSES

2005	2006	2007
2,000	2,200	2,600
13.3 percent	13.3 percent	14.4 percent

OPERATING INCOME MANAGEMENT

OPERATING PROFIT

2005	2006	2007
2,250	2,700	3,200
15.0 percent	16.4 percent	17.8 percent

COST OF CAPITAL

2005	2006	2007
1,200	1,220	1,450
10.0 percent	10.0 percent	10.0 percent

NET FIXED ASSETS

2005	2006	2007
10,000	10,000	12,000

RECEIVABLES

2005	2006	2007
2,000	2,200	2,400
48.0 d	48.0 d	48.0 d

INVENTORY

2005	2006	2007
1,000	1,100	1,200
10.8x	10.5x	10.2x

PAYABLES

2005	2006	2007
1,000	1,100	1,100
48.0 d	49.5 d	48.9 d

WORKING CAPITAL

2005	2006	2007
2,000	2,200	2,500

OPERATING ASSET MANAGEMENT

CAPITAL EMPLOYED

2005	2006	2007
12,000	12,200	14,500
1.4x	1.4x	1.2x

- Can be used to convince upper management to streamline some of the costs centers like purchasing.

Limitations of the Return on Investment model

- The model is based on accounting numbers that may not be reliable.

- The model does not include the cost of capital (remember when rates hit 18 percent — 26 percent).

APPENDIX V
CALCULATING LABOR COSTS

Should you consider your cost of labor to be only the dollar amount per hour paid to Fred?

Consider your payroll taxes as follows in this typical example:

Real Labor Costs

Hourly Rate	$10.00	Hourly Rate	$10.00
Company Portion of CPP at 4.95 percent	$ 0.50	Company Portion of CPP at 4.95 percent	$ 0.50
Company Portion of Employment Insurance	$ 0.25	Company Portion of Employment Insurance	$ 0.25
Vacation, 2 weeks per year (4 percent)	$ 0.40	Vacation, 3 weeks per year (6 percent)	$ 0.60
Benefits	$ 1.00	Benefits	$ 1.00
	$12.15		$12.35
Payroll taxes add 21 percent	$ 2.10	Payroll taxes add 23 percent	$ 2.30

The employee and employer contribution rates for Canada Pension Plan for 2007 are 4.95 percent, and the self-employed contribution rate is unchanged at 9.9 percent (Canada Revenue Agency).

For employees, the premium rate is $1.80 per $100 of insurable earnings, effective January 1, 2007. The rate paid by employers is $2.52 per $100 of insurable earnings (Canada Revenue Agency).

Benefit costs vary depending upon the plan and the portion paid by the employer, but typically run at $1.00 per hour cost to the employer for the plan to be of any value whatsoever.

APPENDIX VI
CALCULATING THE BREAKEVEN

Breakeven Point

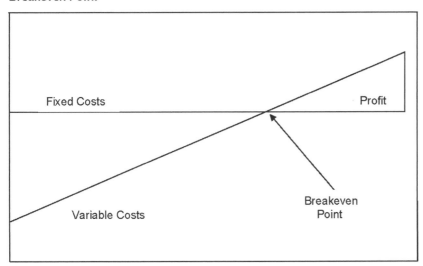

In the above diagram, fixed costs are those things you cannot escape even if the sales volume was $1 for the period. These are rent, heat, light, salaried employees, and insurance, among others. So the line for fixed costs is a straight line.

Variable costs are the costs attributable to the production of each widget. The more widgets you make or the more contract labor you sell, the higher the bill will be for the costs incurred, so the line is angled upwards.

The breakeven point is reached when the profit made on each sale of widgets or contracted labor pays for its own incremental costs plus the variable costs.

Beyond the breakeven point, profit is made because the fixed costs are paid for and the only costs are the inherent cost of producing the good or service.

The importance of knowing your breakeven point is to focus the attention of management and accounting on the fixed costs. Every dollar of fixed costs eliminated reduces the dollar volume of sales needed.

How can I apply this, you say? Well suppose that an employee asks for a pay raise. This will become a fixed cost if you acquiesce. On the other hand, offering a bonus for reaching some target transforms this into a variable cost.

Or consider this diagram from an actual company in the interior of British Columbia that I examined. This diagram converts the sales volumes to days of the year.

Reaching Breakeven

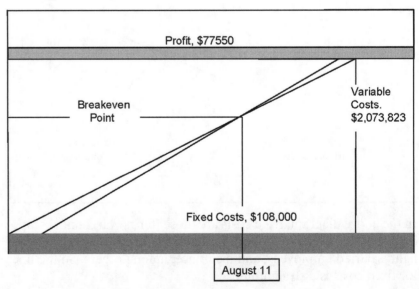

In this diagram, the fixed costs are low. The variable costs are a significant part of the costs. Profit is a tiny 3.43 percent.

In this diagram it is obvious that keeping the fixed costs low means that the profit day comes in the early part of August each year. But the profit numbers are small.

The diagnosis: Either the variable cost of labor and materials is too high or the prices are too low.

APPENDIX VII
CALCULATING HOW MANY EXTRA SALES ARE NEEDED TO OFFSET A PRICE DECREASE

In most companies, there is a struggle between the finance managers who wish to drive costs down and prices up, while marketing wishes to drive sales up and prices down. In smaller companies, this struggle takes place in the mind of the single owner.

SCENARIO 1:

WITH NO CHANGE IN VARIABLE OR FIXED COST, WHAT IS THE PRICE/VOLUME TRADE-OFF?

In this example we have left fixed and variable costs alone in order to facilitate an easier calculation. Most price decreases are undertaken on the assumption that a price drop will generate huge sales and therefore huge profits. Here is the math to enable the business owner to calculate what sales volume is required to offset this decrease and to help set targets for sales staff.

OLDCO Company is considering a 5 percent price cut which will change the price from $9.95 to $9.45 for each bucket of doggie biscuits and thus make itself more competitive within its trading area. Marketing believes that they will be able to sell 20 percent more. The operations manager believes that variable costs will not have to increase in response to this pricing decision — i.e., the company will not have to look for cheaper raw materials.

If only the price changes, this will cause profit to fall from $30,000 to $25,000. This is called the price effect and is the basis for a price decision.

Price Effect

Sales in Units	10,000	10,000	11,250
Price per Unit	$ 9.95	$ 9.45	$ 9.45
Revenue Total	$99,500.00	$94,500.00	$106,313.00
Variable Costs per unit	$ 5.45	$ 5.45	$ 5.45
Gross Margin per unit	$ 4.50	$ 4.00	$ 4.00
Total Gross Margin	$45,000.00	$40,000.00	$ 45,000.00
Fixed Costs	$15,000.00	$15,000.00	$ 15,000.00
Profit	$30,000.00	$25,000.00	$ 30,000.00

To offset this profit collapse, how many more buckets of doggie biscuits will have to be sold?

How Much Do You Need to Sell?

NEW VOLUME =

$$\text{NEW VOLUME} = \frac{\text{EXPECTED PROFIT} + \text{FIXED COSTS}}{\text{NEW GROSS MARGIN}}$$

$$NV = \frac{\$30,000 + \$15,000}{\$4} = \$11,250$$

SCENARIO 2:

WITH A CHANGE IN VARIABLE COST, WHAT IS THE PRICE/VOLUME TRADE-OFF?

In this example we have left fixed costs alone and allowed for a change in variable costs in order to reflect a declining cost of production or, in the case of distributor or retailer, a drop in unit price due to a larger commitment. In this instance, the cost to make or buy a unit will drop the more you buy, or the more you make. In this marketing plan, price decreases are undertaken on the assumption that a price drop will generate a temporary drop in margins followed by huge sales and therefore huge profits. This is the math to enable the business owner to calculate what sales volume is required to offset this decrease and to help set targets for sales staff.

Offsetting a Price Decrease

	Now	Price Effect	New Volumes Required
Sales in Units	10,000	10,000	11,268
Price per Unit	$ 9.95	$ 9.45	$ 9.45
Revenue Total	$99,500.00	$94,500.00	$106,479.00
Variable Costs per Unit	$ 5.45	$ 5.45	$ 5.45
Gross Margin per Unit	$ 4.50	$ 4.00	$ 4.00
Total Gross Margin	$45,000.00	$40,000.00	$ 45,070.00
Fixed Costs	$15,000.00	$15,000.00	$ 15,000.00
Profit	$30,000.00	$25,000.00	$ 30,070.00

OLDCO Company is considering a 5 percent price cut which will change the price from $9.95 to $9.45 and thus make itself more competitive within its trading area. Marketing believes that they will be able to sell 20 percent more. The operations manager believes that variable costs can be cut by 20 cents by substituting raw, fresh carrots in the dog biscuits with frozen carrots.

Cutting Variable Costs

Change in Variable Costs Only	Now	Price Effect	Sales Needed
Sales in Units	10,000	10,000	11,714
Price per Unit	$ 9.95	$ 9.45	$ 9.45
Revenue Total	$99,500.00	$94,500.00	$106,247.00
Variable Costs per Unit	$ 5.45	$ 5.45	$ 5.25
Gross Margin per Unit	$ 4.50	$ 4.20	$ 4.20
Total Gross Margin	$45,000.00	$42,000.00	$ 44,998.80
Fixed Costs	$15,000.00	$15,000.00	$ 15,000.00
Profit	$30,000.00	$27,000.00	$ 29,999.00

In the first column (now) this is the situation with fixed costs at $15,000, variable costs at $5.45 per unit and profit at $30,000.

In the second column, only the price has changed which will drive down profits by $5,000. This is called the price effect because price is the only variable altered and we need to see that impact in order to create a baseline.

In the third column we have used the formula below to calculate how much extra volume is required at the new prices to keep the profit figure the same.

Calculating Extra Volume

NEW VOLUME =   EXPECTED PROFIT + FIXED COSTS
                 ─────────────────────────────────
                        NEW GROSS MARGIN

NV = EP + FC
     ─────────
        NGM

NV = $30,000.00 + $15,000.00   = $11,714.00
     ──────────────────────────
            $4.20

SCENARIO 3

WITH A CHANGE IN FIXED COST AND VARIABLE COST, WHAT IS THE PRICE/VOLUME TRADE-OFF?

In some instances, fixed costs can change too, and that will affect the price and the sales volume needed to offset a price drop. As already hinted above in the discussion on capacity utilization, as a plant nears full capacity costs can increase: overtime to meet tight deadlines, maintenance frequency increases, etc.

In this example, the price has been dropped as before, the frozen carrots have been ground up and a new invoicing agent has been hired at the rate of $2,000 per month, adding to the fixed costs.

Calculating the Tradeoff

NEW VOLUME =   EXPECTED PROFIT + FIXED COSTS
                 ─────────────────────────────────
                        NEW GROSS MARGIN

NV = EP + FC
     ─────────
        NGM

NV = $30,000.00 + $17,000.00   = $11,190.00
     ──────────────────────────
            $4.20

Price/Volume Tradeoff

Change in Variable Costs Only	Now	Price Effect	Sales Needed
Sales in Units	10,000	10,000	11,190
Price per Unit	$ 9.95	$ 9.45	$ 9.45
Revenue Total	$99,500.00	$94,500.00	$105,746.00
Variable Costs per Unit	$ 5.45	$ 5.45	$ 5.25
Gross Margin per Unit	$ 4.50	$ 4.20	$ 4.20
Total Gross Margin	$45,000.00	$42,000.00	$ 46,998.80
Fixed Costs	$15,000.00	$17,000.00	$ 17,000.00
Profit	$30,000.00	$25,000.00	$ 29,998.00

APPENDIX VIII
READING LIST

Ahmed, Ted and El Basha, Hanan. "Heterogeneity of Consumer Demand: Opportunities for pricing services." Journal Of Products and Brand Management; 2006. Vol. 15, Issue 4/5.

Baker. Ronald J. *Pricing on Purpose. Creating and Capturing Value.* John Wiley and Sons Inc. Hoboken, NJ. 2006

Bergfeld, C. Daniel. *Strategic Pricing. Protecting profit margins from inflation.* AMA Management Briefing. New York, NY. 1981

Bernstein, Jerry. "The Secrets to Price-Setting." Business Week Online. 11.6.2006.

Calogridis, Michael. "What are the minimum requirements to enable a successful pricing strategy?" Journal of Revenue and Pricing Management; Oct 2006, Vol. 5, Issue 3

Cokins, Gary. "Are All of Your Customers Profitable? A Technical bulletin from ABC Technologies." Beaverton, OR. 1999

Daly, John L. *Pricing for Profitability: Activity-based Pricing for Competitive Advantage.* John Wiley and Sons. New York, NY. 2002.

De Rose, Louis. "Value Selling. The strategy for: reaching the industrial customer, Satisfying customer requirements, competing in cost-conscious markets." American Management Association. New York, 1989.

Dettmer, William H. *Goldratt's Theory of Constraints: A Systems Approach to Continuous Improvement*. ASQ Quality Press. Milwaukee, WI. 1997.

Docters, Rob. "Bundles with Sharp Teeth: Effective product combinations." Journal of Business Strategy ; 2006, Vol. 27, Issue 5.

Dunne, David. "Wicked by Design" Marketing Magazine; 7/31/2006, Vol 3, Issue 26.

Garbato, Debbie. "A Destination for Cherry Pitters" Retail Merchandiser, May 2006, Vol.46. Issue 5.

Ford, Henry. *My Life and Work*. New York, Doubleday, Page & Company. 1923.

Gerber, Michael E. *The E-myth: Why Most Businesses Don't Work and What to Do About It*. Harper Business. New York, NY. 1986.

Goldratt Eliyahu M., Jeff Cox. *The Goal: A Process of Ongoing Improvement*. North River Press, Barrington, MA. 1992.

Landsburg, Steven E. *The Armchair Economist: Economics and Everyday Life*. The Free Press, Simon & Schuster. New York, NY. 1993

Leavitt, Theodore. "Marketing Myopia." Harvard Business Review. No. 75507. September-October, 1975.

Marn, Michael V. and Robert L. Rosiello. "Managing price, gaining Profit." Harvard Business Review. Sept-Oct. 1992.

Nagle, T.E. and Hogan, E. H. *The Strategy and Tactics of Pricing. A Guide to Growing More Profitably*. Prentice Hall, Pearson Education Inc. Upper Saddle River, NJ. 2006.

Puty, Claudio Castelo Branco. "Cost Curves and Capacity Utilization in the U.S. Manufacturing, 1958-1996." Department of Economics, Universidade Federal do Pará. Belém, Brazil. 2005.

Ross, Elliot B. "Making Money with Proactive Pricing." Harvard Business Review. No. 84614. November-December, 1984.

Schragenheim, Eli. *Management Dilemmas: The Theory of Constraints Approach to Problem Identification and Solutions*. CRC Press LLC. Boca Raton, FL. 1999.

Shapiro, Benson P. and Barbara B. Jackson. "Industrial Pricing to meet customer needs." Harvard Business Review. No.78609. November-December, 1978.

Winkler, John. *Pricing for Results.* Butterworth-Heinemann. London, UK. 1983.

Berndt, E. and J. Morrison. "Capacity utilization measures: Underlying Economic Theory and an Alternative Approach," American Economic Review, pp. 48-52, 2:71, May 1981.

I. Johanson. "Production functions and the concept of capacity." Collection Economie et Mathematique et Econometrie, 2, 1968, pp. 46-72.

Perelman, Michael. *Keynes, Investment Theory and the Economic Slowdown: The Role of Replacement Investment and Q-Ratios.* Palgrave Macmillan. New York, NY. 1989.

Strange, Susan and Roger Tooze. *The International Politics of Surplus Capacity: Competition for Market Shares in the World Recession.* Unwin Hyman. London, UK. 1982.

Crotty, James. "Why there is chronic excess capacity - The Market Failures Issue." Challenge, Nov-Dec, 2002.

Rawski,Thomas G. "The Political Economy of China's Declining Growth." University of Pittsburgh. 1999.

Shaikh, Anwar and Jamee Moudud. "Measuring Capacity Utilization in OECD Countries: A Cointegration Method." Levy Economics Institute, Working Paper No. wp415. November 2004.

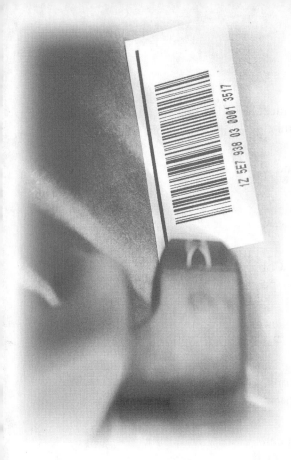

APPENDIX IX
WEBSITES

12manage
http://www.12manage.com/methods_dupont_model.html

Description of the DuPont Model of financial analysis
Louis De Rose
http://www.circuitree.com/CDA/Articles
May require paid subscription

The Donald Cooper Corporation
http://www.donaldcooper.com/pages/home.htm

John Winkler
http://www.thewinklers.co.uk/business/index.htm
Winkler offers seminars and pricing tips